SWEET TEMPTATIONS

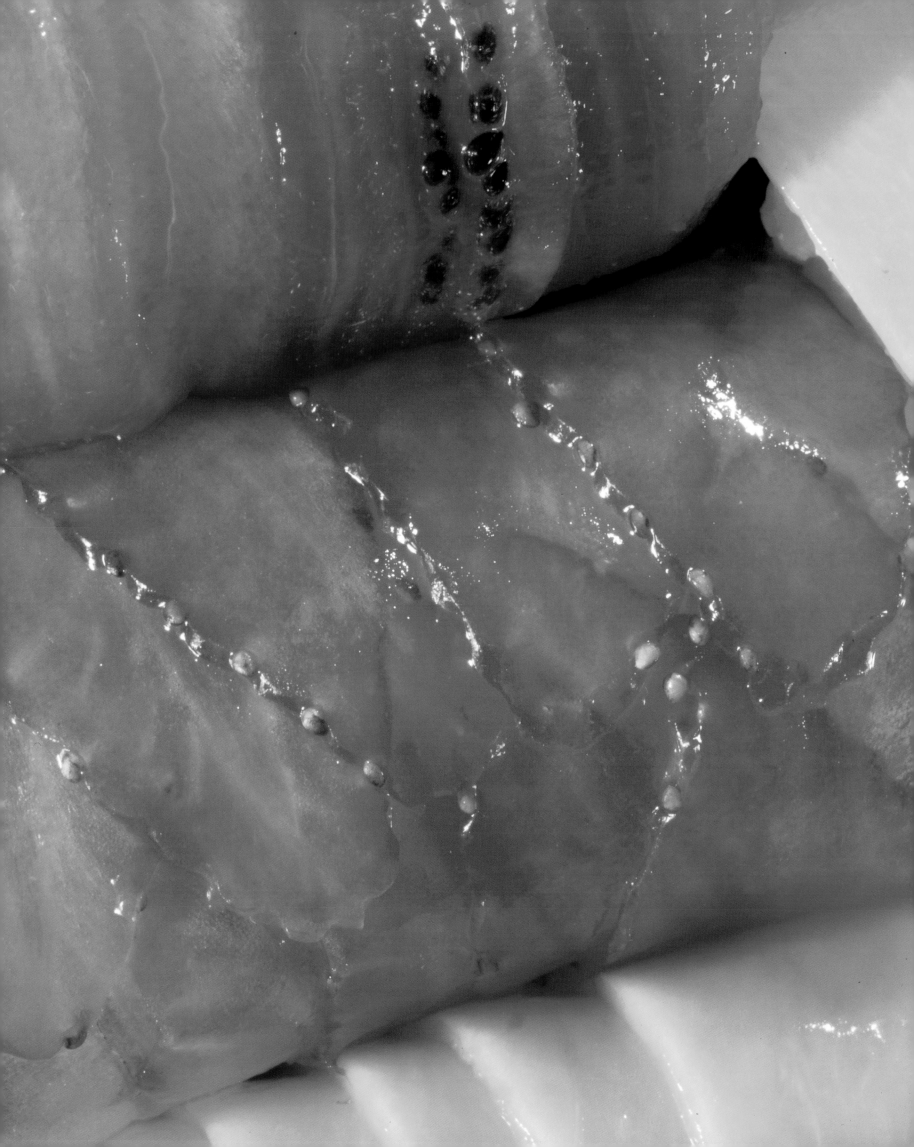

SWEET TEMPTATIONS

Created, produced and written by
MARÍA VILLEGAS

Designed and edited by
BENJAMÍN VILLEGAS

Photography
MATTHEW LEIGHTON

Villegas
editores

This book has been created, produced and
published in Colombia by,
© VILLEGAS EDITORES 1998
Avenida 82 No. 11-50, Interior 3
e-mail: villegas@colomsat.net.co
Telephone (57-1) 616 1788. Fax (57-1) 616 0020
Bogotá, D.C., Colombia.

Layout
MERCEDES CEDEÑO

Style revision
AMY ALBERT
STELLA DE FEFERBAUM

Glossary and indexes
MARCELLA ECHAVARRIA

Illustrations
DANIELA MEJÍA

English translation
ANDREW ALEXANDER REID

First Edition
October 1998

ISBN
958-9393-51-9

Jacket, Cherries with Roquefort and walnut ice cream
Back jacket, Kahlua chocolates with raspberries
    and phyllo
Page 1, Millefeuille of crispy apples, iced saffron
    cream and caramel
Page 2/3, Chocolate biscuit
Page4, Fruit sushi with lychee rice
Page 7, Baked plums

Villegas, María
    Sweet temptations / Created, produced and written by
María Villegas ; Photography Matthew Leighton ; Translator
Andrew Alexander Reid ; Glossary and indexes Marcella
Echavarría ; Illustrations Daniela Mejía; Director, designer
and editor Benjamín Villegas. -- Bogotá : Villegas, 1998.
    200 p. : ill. col. ; 31 x 25 cm.
    Includes indexes and appendixes
    Original title : Dulce tentación
    ISBN 958-9393-51-9

1. Desserts 2. Confectionery 3. Cuisine I. Tit. II. Leighton,
Matthew, phot. III. Reid, Andrew Alexander, tr. IV. Mejía,
Daniela, ill. V. Villegas, Benjamín, ed.

641.86 CDD
TX773 LC

To Andrés, with all my love

Contents

The unusual 26

The ethnic 58

Foreword

Pastry-making: An exact science!

María Villegas, a painstaking perfectionist, formerly a young student at our Le Cordon Bleu School in Paris, could not have done better in her first work *Sweet Temptations.* Here she gives us startling gourmet recipes which are purely her creation, startling for their brazen intelligence and creative lucidity.

María has flung the gauntlet and will enthrall even the most delicate and refined palates. Amateurs and professionals alike, we will find in this book the most daring combinations of flavors infused with subtlety; flavors that are sweet, of course, but orchestrated like a musical score where the balance of mixtures proves a marvelous alchemy, blending acidity and spices with crunchy and melting textures.

María's first encounter with "Dame Gastronomie" did not occur all that long ago; it was when she attended the classes I was giving during a stay in Bogotá. Who would have thought then that she would now be giving us lessons in pure creativity, worthy of the world's greatest pastry chefs?

This work reveals an innate sense of perfection. It shows with great clarity that in any part of the world, observation and intelligence are enough for concocting gastronomic marvels from known and common ingredients to sweep us off into a gustatory world beyond our wildest imagination.

Let us allow ourselves to be transported by this work and enter the game that María wants us to play. It is the work of a true lover of culinary art. One of the future great masters of gastronomy, María has not yet finished to surprise us, and, like me, readers will be captivated by her talent. With *Sweet Temptations* she confirms her respect for professionalism in the highest sense of the word.

Thank you María, and continue your good work, for you have left us eager for more. "Even if a little mystery is left," to quote your own words, María, "in Mona Lisa's beautiful smile, so difficult to define," we, on the contrary, wish to penetrate all the mysteries of your creations in your next works.

Patrick Terrien
Chef des Chefs
Le Cordon Bleu, Paris

Amaretto *aspic*

Introduction

In their simple daily actions, all human beings are creative. What transforms someone into an artistically creative person depends on genes and circumstances that endowed such a creative gift. In my case, the circumstances were fortunate. I grew up in a a family sensitive to beauty, surrounded by beautiful objects and books of exquisite design. I was also fortunate to live in a climate of independence where my decisions were respected.

Since my earliest childhood, I was able to give free rein to a creative vocation without having to let practical considerations guide my career choice. So often people tend to choose that which is most useful rather than explore that which slumbers in the depths of their sensitivity. I could have chosen to become a psychologist, a fashion designer, or a *chef de cuisine,* and could have funneled into one of these activities the potential for creativity that I felt within me. I chose cuisine.

I once read a short story by Isak Dinesen (Karen Blixen), in which a woman, who was a famous cook at a grand restaurant in Paris, was forced at a time of social turmoil to flee the city and abandon a prestigious career. She emigrated to a bleak, austere northern country, foreign to the pleasures of the table and to the creative inclinations which had been the purpose of her life. She could not imagine being anything other than a cook but in exile she was prevented from following her profession. However, one day, she enjoyed an unexpected stroke of luck; with a lottery ticket she won the jackpot. She then decided to cook a banquet for the people in the village where she ilived. The local people were ignorant of the pleasures of the table and found any extravagance reprehensible. The woman prepared the banquet in order to give the best of herself, to show generosity and also in order to offer these austere folks a pleasure of which they had until then had no inkling.

The story moved me deeply. Against all odds this woman remained the great cook she had once been. Her pleasure lay in her capacity not only to create but in offering the results of her creativity to others. Something of this was part of my decision to devote myself to cooking. I do it for pleasure, for the need to focus my intuitions, and for the satisfaction of offering the product of my work to others.

It was not a strange choice. My mother and grandmothers had sublimated home cooking into something beyond routine. They were not satisfied merely with cooking succulent dishes. They also had to present them to please the eye. As a little girl, I had already learned that cooking was a creative vehicle, and not only a way of satisfying the appetite. I had

Chef María Villegas

learned that cooking and life had rituals and rules in common that are prominent in every culture and that individuals and societies distinguish themselves by them.

My decision to devote myself to cooking came about because cooking was something with which I had become familiar. I began to see the possibility of taking it a step further, to confer on it a wider scope. I wanted to explore multiple possibilities through a variety of styles, through the characteristics adopted from one culture into another, from one country into another, and through the influences exerted by mixing customs and racial preferences.

I realized that intuition must be tempered by apprenticeship and I had the great fortune to attend a special class given by Patrick Terrien in Bogotá. This encounter with Terrien marked the beginning of a friendship and it also marked my definitive entrance into the professional study of *haute cuisine.*

Where should I seek such academic knowledge? Which school enjoyed the greatest prestige? Without a shadow of doubt it was the Cordon Bleu in Paris, the holiest of holy sanctuaries in Western cuisine. There, I again enjoyed the privilege of meeting Terrien, who not only was one of my teachers but also became a close friend who, with tremendous generosity and affection, guided, stimulated and advised me throughout my studies. It is a great honor for me that Terrien agreed to write the foreword for this book

With similar good fortune, I got to know the restaurant *El Bulli* in Rosas on the Costa Brava and its chef Ferrán Adriá. It proved to be an unmitigated revelation, as if, after seeing the paintings of the Renaissance, I had discovered the disconcerting and boundless genius of Picasso. Not only did Adriá know what he was doing but he had also expressed a theory of his personal concept of cuisine. To me he was, and remains to this day, an eminent example of creativity.

"To create new dishes," Adriá writes in his book, "we start from a composite art." The three elements are, according to him, essential to the formation of new criteria, quite different from the important academic criteria that I had learned at the Cordon Bleu. These are: inspiration, adaptation, and association. "Inspiration," explains Adriá, "activated the impact triggered by a determined non-culinary element, a work of art for instance. Adaptation means the rethinking of an already existent dish. By association I understand the concoction of a dish based on several elements suggested in an almost random manner."

Rose petals for garnish

14

The theories of this great chef were decisive in my training, and not only as theories since I was able to see how he systematically put them into practice. Adriá's theories lead to another conclusion: random choice presupposes that a diversity exists, that a chef worth his salt can use. To the same extent that one learns the basic rules of cuisine, it is essential to get to know other culinary traditions: the diversity, the points in commonn, the differences and peculiarities, and the influences that enrich them.

I set out to learn about this variety on the spot and traveled to those cities and countries where cuisine had always enjoyed a mark of prestige. I carried with me the seed of creative rebellion that Adriá had instilled in me as well as a tremendous respect for the authority of the *Cordon Bleu.*

There has always been cultural dialogue between the West and the East. Cuisine is also part of this dialogue. The cuisines of Europe and the cuisines of Asia "talk to each other" and influence each other while preserving their peculiarities. I believe that more often than not, the term "international cuisine" is an overstatement. It generally, it refers to a cuisine international only on a European scale.

In France, Spain, Italy, the United States, Thailand, Hong Kong, Singapore, Vietnam and Australia I formed a good part of my universal vision of cuisine. I adopted what interested me and rejected that which did not. My purpose was to make something new, to learn and to create, to transcend things learned through a random method. I began to approach the area of experimentation and creation in the preparation of desserts.

Innovation

When I am asked if I seek innovation in traditional desserts, my answer is positive. This is the sole object of this book along with my obsessive effort to create alternatives to what is already known and accepted. Inevitably there will be questions about this book, to what extent it is special or original. Does it represent a contribution and an example? I hope that this book will find its place on the shelves of kitchens and libraries alike. My publisher and I invested all our efforts in this work. It is a book to be looked at, whether one likes to cook or not. With my recipes and these photogrphs I seek to stimulate the readers' appetite and imagination.

I believe that there are unusual and surprising combinations of ingredients that function perfectly well together and that there are common combinations, generally used in appetizers and entrees, which work equally well in desserts. I also believe that a gourmet, just as an artist, is in spirit more open to curiosity about the new than satisfied by the norm. This

Tangerine in anise syrup

book may be unsettling to conservative and traditional gastronomic sensitivities, but then it is not compiled to please them. I wish to make an amiable challenge: dare! If the taste and aspect please you, go on, step merrily away from the beaten path, and share this adventure with me.

I am aware that many chefs may object to what is written here, not in the form but in the content. I can assure them that I am in earnest. Obviously I cannot describe flavors. Nonetheless, throughout these recipes I meet the challenge. What is presented here is feasible and it provides satisfying results. Try these recipes, take at least a nibble! The desserts may look complex but they are not so difficult to prepare. I made several in one afternoon.

You may ask: "why such concern with subtlety, texture and color?" My answer is that I have observed too little concern for these elements. Recently more emphasis has been paced particularly on presentation. My concern lies equally in visual harmony and in the pleasant surprise offered by subtlety of flavor.

Another important thing for me is the blend of textures. No one has ever pointed it out to me, and it is for this reason that I attempt to emphasize the textures of the desserts as strongly as possible. I always combine a minimum of two textures in the same dessert and I adore playing with temperatures —a variant overlooked by most chefs.

I also believe that pastry cooking is going in the direction I am pointing and I am sure that every good restaurant is heading in the same direction. Food critics have began to pay close attention to the last chapter of a meal, as if they acknowledge that it is just as important to say *au revoir* as *bonjour* at the table. As a consequence, pastry chefs have begun to rise to a privileged rank.

The pleasure of eating desserts

The best part of a dessert is the mixture of flavors, aromas and textures. This is how I feel, and what I propose to demonstrate in this book. The point is to achieve harmony in subtlety. I wouldn't go so far as saying that these desserts represent the essential conclusion to a meal, or that they should accompany such or such a dish. These desserts go with any type of dish and the final choice depends on one's appetite; delicate taste is the factor instead of what normally determines the choice of dessert, the feeling that one has "eaten well."

Aromas have always had a great effect on me and it is a subject over which I like to linger. Personally I am endowed with an excellent memory of

Herb and flower essences

smells, as had the hero of *Perfume*, Patrick Süskind's spicy novel, but in a different field. I associate people with smells and scents. I could say that I have little memory for people's names and faces but I remember their smell just as I remember the aroma of the food each time I eat something. For the same reason, essences and flowers hold such fascination for me: nards, jasmines, orange blossoms —aromas that I introduce into some of my desserts.

Forms and colors

Colors are fundamental for me. They are an essential aspect, not a mere accessory in all my desserts. I maintain that colors play an important role in stimulating appetite. They may whet or spoil it. One can observe the growing importance of color in restaurants: in the table linen, the menu, in wall shades, plates and dishes. Therefore it is not absurd to say that there are edible and delicious colors as well as colors capable of causing the adverse effect: spoiling the appetite.

When jotting down my market list, I am in the habit of noting colors. If I jump out of bed in the morning after a yellow dream, I make a beeline for oranges and lemons. If the morning theme is red, it will be strawberries and plums. Depending on the day, market availability will decide the predominant colors of my desserts.

If subtlety of taste seems fundamental to me, the same applies for the presentation and finish that would be incomplete without the final touch. I use a minimum of colorings and infrequently at that. I prefer the natural colors of the raw materials. The main thing is to preserve the natural element and above all not to conceal or blur it.

The creation process and form

I adore toying with form. Form is part of the creative process. I always look back at my childhood, free of constraint and set patterns. Children play with form, and many of the great artists of the twentieth century have followed their example in an attempt to recover innocence and freedom. In this manner I surrender to my instinct and give free rein to intuition, while not forgetting apprenticeship.

In the process of writing this book, I made up some new recipes that did not work out. If I had to sum up my method, I would say that my first step is to walk down to the market or open the refrigerator. Raw materials immediately at hand determine the form and content of a dish. When an ingredient comes to mind, I immediately think of what could accompany it,

Caramelized macadamia nuts

and I get a sense of what the final result should be. The fragrance and texture of each ingrediet must be present in the final product, for the palate as well as for the olfactory sense. In the same way, the form that I give to the desert must have visual impact.

My aim is to make it possible to distinguish the taste of each ingredient within the symphony of the final product and to avoid elements that neutralize each other. However varied, ingredients must keep their own identity within the dessert.

Forms merge from visual perception and imagination. They are born from other existent forms, but submitted to a subtle and coherent modification. One can start from what exists and transform it. I could give many examples, each reflecting a process of adaptation to make things different through imagination.

My major concern has always been to create suggestive and creative forms without yielding to the temptation of facility. The presentation of the desserts in this book is their visual identity. I would like readers to realize their creative possibilities. This has been my intention ever since I began to plan this book, assisted by my dear friend Katrina Markoff, to whom I express my gratitude and friendship.

I maintain profound respect for classical recipes. It would be just as impossible to hide my debt towards them as to hide the additional touches I have given in order to compile this book. This is the fruit of a free and spontaneous will to create a collection of recipes in the most artistic manner I am capable of.

"Do not sing to the rose, make it blossom in a poem," wrote Chilean poet Vicente Huidrobo. "Do not sing to desserts," if I may paraphrase these verses, "use your imagination to create them." This is what I proposed to myself, and I continue to do so.

María Villegas

The author, María Villegas, with the photographer, Matthew Leighton, during photography production for the book

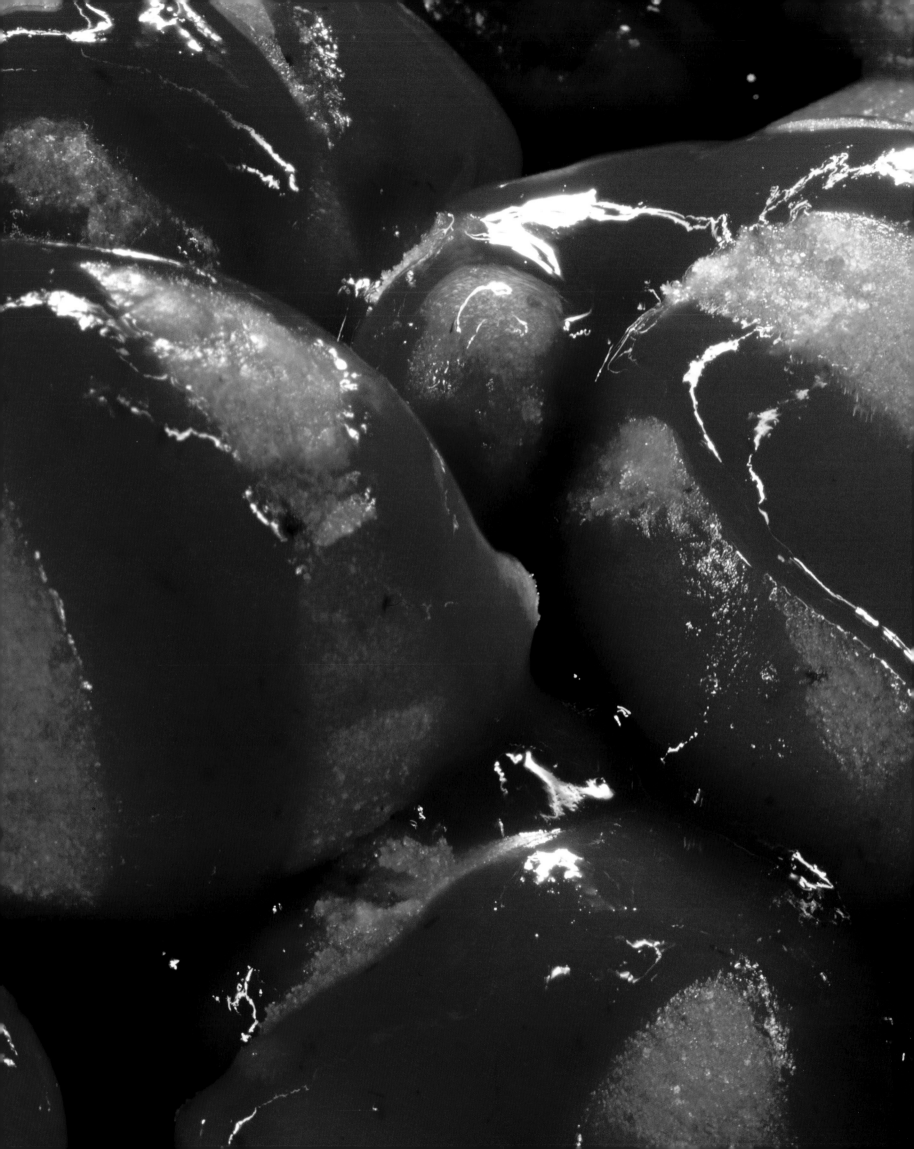

Recommendations

How to use this book

The recipes in this book are divided into four parts: ingredients, preparation, presentation and special equipment.

The first part provides a complete list of the ingredients for the dessert. In a few cases, some ingredients appear as a separate recipe included in the Appendix at the end of this book.

The second part consists of a detailed explanation enabling any person with a basic knowledge of cooking to prepare the desserts. In some cases, the text is accompanied by sketches to clarify the more complex steps.

The third part is dedicated to presentation of the desserts in order to serve them as they appear in the accompanying photographs.

The fourth part consists of a list of utensils. These are not necessarily found in every kitchen but they are essential for the successful preparation of each recipe.

Before starting preparation of any dessert in this book, it is imperative to read the complete recipe, in order to become familiarized with it and be sure to have all the necessary ingredients and equipment at hand. One must follow strictly the order of different preparations involved in a certain dessert, as they have been organized according to the time they take.

A glossary of terms is found on page 186. Words defined in the glossary are given in *italics* the first time they appear in a recipe, except for titles and captions. Illustrations of the utensils most used in the book appear on page 188.

Measures and temperatures

All the recipes in this book were created and developed for sea level and are valid up to an altitude of 3600 feet. At higher altitudes, it is necessary to make some modifications to ingredients and oven temperature.

Liquids: For each cup of liquid, one must add two tablespoons up to 5400 feet above sea level and four tablespoons higher up.

Sugar: For each cup of sugar, one must reduce the quantity to 7/8 of a cup up to 5400 feet above sea level and to 3/4 of a cup higher up.

Yeast and baking powder: Each teaspoon of yeast or baking powder must be reduced by half up to 5400 feet above sea level and by three quarters higher up.

Oven temperature: Oven temperature must be increased from three to five degrees Fahrenheit every 1000 feet over 5400 feet above sea level.

Strawberry sorbet with raspberry coulis

L autréamont, the great French poet of
Uruguayan origin, wrote that poetry was the
meeting between an umbrella and a sewing-
machine. Lewis Carroll's masterful work *Alice in
Wonderland,* gave *nonsense* its full meaning, in
other words, that which apparently makes no sense.
Alice goes through the mirror and enters the
fascinating and outlandish world of adventure,
where the unusual prevails over the sense of reality.

From time immemorial, art has embodied the
struggle to break the habits of perception, ''the
great habit,'' as Julio Cortázar said. Mystery swirls
around habit to break it, as in the paintings of De
Chirico and Magritte. All arts, among which cuisine
is one of the most ancient, are supreme efforts of
creativity, searching for combinations, for the
balance between sweet and salty, raw and cooked,
warm and cold.

To imagine the unusual in this series of desserts
is, in short, a creative adventure, the adventure of
the unexpected. What could not be imagined as

compatible proves to be compatible. These desserts are an exercise in creation aimed at the senses. They surprise with a previously unimaginable encounter or mixture. Flavors produce a communion which, besides being pleasant, leads the taster to ponder over the origin of the elements he is tasting. He distinguishes them and unites them in that new, unusual, unexpected taste of which he had been deprived by habit.

For sure, this is not the "encounter between the umbrella and the sewing - machine." It is a less absurd and less symbolic encounter between grapes and passion fruit, between cherries and *Roquefort* cheese, between apple and saffron, between chocolate and beet. Finally, it is an encounter of elements that habit and a somewhat conservative concept of cuisine had never imagined together. It is also the practical and at the same time playful sense of creation: to pass through the mirror of tastes is equivalent to uniting them in a concert of "instruments" that have figured in no score.

Coimbra

Port and grape jelly with granadilla

4 servings

Ingredients

Grape jelly
- 3 leaves gelatin
- 2 cups port
- ½ cup light syrup, see Appendix, page 181
- 1 cup black seedless grapes

Tuiles
- 1 oz butter
- ¼ cup confectioners' sugar
- ½ cup port
- ⅓ cup sifted flour

Garnish
- 4 *granadillas*
- 4 bunches black grapes

Special equipment
- kitchen scales
- measuring cup
- 4 metal rings, 5cm in diameter and 3cm high
- pastry bag
- *silpat* sheet

Preparation

Grape jelly

Soak the gelatin in iced water until softened.

Boil the port in a saucepan until reduced to one and a half cups. Add the syrup and mix well. Drain the gelatin and dissolve it in a little warm water and add it to the port mixture. To make a bottom for the rings, place each ring on a piece of plastic wrap, pressing the excess wrap around the outer surface. Place the rings on a sheet pan and fill each ring with the jelly mixture. Distribute the seedless grapes in the rings and chill until the jelly firms.

Tuiles

In a saucepan over low heat, melt the butter, add the sugar and stir well. Beat until creamy. In a second saucepan, boil the port until reduced to three tablespoons. Gradually stir in the flour. Beat until the batter is combined and smooth. Cover with plastic wrap and chill for at least an hour.

Preheat the oven to 300°F/150°C.

With a pastry bag, pipe equal portions of batter onto a silpat sheet or onto a greased and floured sheet pan, leaving a 10cm space between each portion.

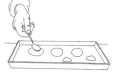

With the back of a spoon, spread each portion into rounds of 8cm in diameter. To keep the dough from sticking to the back of the spoon, dip the spoon in cold water as necessary. Bake for 6 to 8 minutes or until the *tuiles* brown. Remove from oven and cool.

Presentation

Place a tuile on each plate. Unmold the jellies, setting one on each tuile. Slice open the granadillas and pour the pulp over the jellies. Garnish with a bunch of grapes and serve.

Paraná

Starfruit with parsley parfait

4 servings

Ingredients

Parsley parfait
- ½ leaf gelatin
- 1 cup milk
- 1 cup parsley leaves
- 2 egg yolks
- ⅛ cup sugar
- ½ cup heavy cream

Parsley syrup
- ¼ cup water
- ¼ cup sugar
- ¼ cup parsley leaves

Starfruit
- 4 *starfruits*

Special equipment
- measuring cup
- sheet pan

Preparation

Parsley parfait

Soak the gelatin in iced water until softened.

Simmer the milk with the parsley for five minutes. Remove from heat, cool for 15 minutes, and strain, discarding the parsley.

In a separate bowl, beat the egg yolks with the sugar until pale and creamy. Reheat the milk. Then slowly whisk it into the beaten eggs. Hot milk will scramble eggs if this is done too fast. Transfer the mixture to a heavy-duty saucepan, and cook over low heat. Stir constantly with a wooden spoon, taking care not to boil, until the foam disappears from the surface and the mixture coats the back of the spoon. Add the strained gelatin to the hot mixture and beat until completely dissolved. Strain into a bowl set over an ice bath; cool until thickened. Beat the cream until it forms soft peaks, and fold gently into the custard. Cover with plastic wrap, and refrigerate until firm.

Parsley syrup

Boil the water with the sugar until the sugar dissolves. Add the parsley; simmer over low heat for five minutes. Remove from heat, purée in the blender and strain. Refrigerate the syrup.

Starfruit

Wash the starfruit and cut in 2mm thick slices.

Presentation

Arrange two towers on each plate. Use three stars for each plate, layering the stars with a little parsley *parfait*. Drizzle with a ribbon of syrup; garnish with a sprig of parsley on the side.

Tasmania

Eucalyptus ice cream with sugared nard

8 servings

Ingredients

Eucalyptus ice cream

- 2 cups milk
- 1 tablespoon eucalyptus extract
- 5 egg yolks
- $^3/_4$ cup sugar
- 1 cup heavy cream

Sugared flowers

- 1 egg white
- 8 fresh nard flowers
- 16 fresh violet flowers
- 2 tablespoons sugar

Special equipment

- measuring cup
- ice cream maker
- pastry bag
- waxed paper

Preparation

Eucalyptus ice cream

In a saucepan, heat the milk and eucalyptus extract just until boiling. Remove from heat. In a separate bowl, beat the egg yolks with the sugar until pale and creamy. Add half the cream and mix well. Slowly whisk the hot eucalyptus-flavored milk into the egg and sugar mixture. Transfer to a heavy-duty saucepan and cook over low heat. Stir constantly with a wooden spoon, without letting boil, until the foam disappears from the surface and the mixture coats the back of the spoon.

Remove from heat and strain into a bowl set over an ice bath. Add the remaining cream and mix well. Chill thoroughly in the refrigerator. Pour into an ice cream maker and process according to manufacturer's directions. Store in the freezer until serving.

Sugared flowers

Preheat the oven to 300°F/150°C. Line a sheet pan with waxed paper. In a small bowl, beat the egg white with a fork until light and foamy. Brush the nard and violet flowers with the beaten egg white and sprinkle with sugar. Place the sugared flowers on the lined sheet pan and bake for 15 minutes or until dry and lightly golden. Remove from oven and allow to cool.

Presentation

With a pastry bag or an ice cream scoop, portion the ice cream into serving glasses and garnish with the sugared flowers. Serve immediately.

Provence

Cherries with Roquefort and walnut ice cream

4 servings

Ingredients

Walnut ice cream
- see Appendix, page 185

Tuiles
- 1 oz butter
- ¼ cup confectioners' sugar
- 2 tablespoons honey
- ⅓ cup sifted flour
- 1 tablespoon hot water

Stuffed cherries
- 12 cherries with stems
- 1 oz *Roquefort*
- 1 tablespoon heavy cream

Garnish
- 4 nuts

Special equipment
- kitchen scales
- measuring cup
- ice cream maker
- medium-sized sheet pan
- 15cm template
- waxed paper

Preparation

Walnut ice cream

Prepare the walnut ice cream following the recipe in Appendix.

Tuiles

In a saucepan over low heat, melt the butter. Add the sugar, mix well, and beat until creamy. Slowly add the honey, flour and hot water. Continue beating until batter is smooth. Cover with plastic wrap; chill for at least one hour. Preheat the oven to 300°F/150°C. With a flexible spatula, spread the dough over a *silpat* sheet or a greased and floured sheet pan. Form an even layer no thicker than 2mm. Bake for eight to ten minutes or until brown on top.

Remove and allow to settle for ten seconds. Cut a circular template 15cm in diameter. With a sharp knife and your template, cut four rounds and place each in a bowl that's slightly smaller than the rounds. Allow the *tuile* circles to harden into baskets. The tuiles must be warm for molding. If they have hardened a little while cooling, reheat in the oven for a few seconds, then mold quickly.

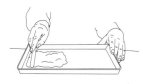

Stuffed cherries

With a paring knife, make an incision at the bottom of each cherry and remove the pit, taking care not to split the fruit. Mash the Roquefort with a fork, add the cream and mix until soft and creamy. Using a cone of waxed paper as a pastry bag, stuff the cherries with the Roquefort mixture.

Presentation

Fill each of the four tuile baskets with 3 stuffed cherries and the walnut ice cream. Garnish with a walnut and serve immediately.

Haifa

Dill-scented citrus fruit in a sugar nest

4 servings

Ingredients

Fruit
- 2 oranges
- 1 grapefruit
- 2 tangerines
- 2 tablespoons lemon juice
- 1 cup water
- 1 tablespoon sugar
- 2 tablespoons fresh dill
- 2 *anise stars*

Angel hair nests
- 1 cup sugar
- ½ cup water
- 3 tablespoons corn syrup
- vegetable oil for greasing forks

Special equipment
- measuring cup
- candy thermometer

Preparation

Fruit

Peel all the citrus fruit as follows: With a paring knife, cut off both ends of the fruit. Peel the skin and pith, slicing close to the pulp. Slice carefully along each side of each segment, avoiding white membrane and seeds. When all segments have been removed, squeeze the remaining pulp over them to get the extra juices.

In a saucepan, mix the lemon juice, water, sugar, dill and star anise. Heat until boiling. Remove from heat and cool. Steep the fruit in this mixture.

Angel hair nests

Prepare an ice bath.

On a work surface, position two tall tumblers 30cm apart to serve as lateral supports for the sugar threading. In a heavy-duty saucepan, mix the sugar, water, and corn syrup. Cook over low heat until the mixture reaches 250°F/ 121°C or the hard ball stage. Immediately, plunge the bottom of the pan into the ice bath to shock. Working quickly, grease two forks with a little vegetable oil and hold them together in one hand so that they look like a single eight-pronged fork. Dip the forks into the syrup, remove, and, with strong wrist movements, swing swiftly from left to right between the supports to form the toffee threads for the nests. The threads will be suspended between the two lateral supports. Repeat until obtaining enough to mold four nests. If the syrup cools, heat again in bain marie. The syrup is delicate and can crystallize easily during cooking or during the process of preparing angel hair. To avoid this, refrain from stirring or reusing sugar that has already hardened. Angel hair can be prepared a few days ahead and can be stored, unmolded, in an airtight container.

Presentation

Mold the angel hair into 4 nests and put one on each plate. Garnish with the marinated fruit and serve immediately.

Tominé

Tuiles with pink peppercorns, curuba ice cream and blackberry coulis

6 servings

Ingredients

Curuba ice cream
- 14 to 16 *curuba* fruit
- 1 ¹/₃ cups condensed milk

Tuiles
- 5 oz butter
- 1 cup sugar
- 1 cup sifted flour
- ⁷/₈ cup coconut milk, see Appendix, page 179
- 1 teaspoon pink peppercorns

Blackberry coulis
- 3¹/₂ oz blackberries
- 1 tablespoon sugar or to taste

Garnish
- lemongrass leaves
- 6 blackberries, halved

Special equipment
- kitchen scales
- measuring cup
- ice cream maker
- two *silpat* sheets or two 30x40cm
- sheet pans

Preparation

Curuba ice cream

Peel the curubas and purée in the blender, pulsing to avoid crushing the seeds. Strain, discard the seeds and pulp. Measure two cups of curuba juice and mix with the condensed milk. Chill for about half an hour, then process the mixture in an ice cream maker according to the manufacturer's directions. Store in the freezer until using. For best results, process the ice cream as close to serving as possible.

Tuiles

Melt the butter, add the sugar, and beat until creamy. Slowly add the flour and coconut milk; beat until batter is smooth. Cover with plastic wrap and chill for at least an hour. Heat the oven to 300°F/ 150°C. With a flexible spatula, spread the dough over two greased and floured 30x40cm sheet pans, until forming an even layer, no thicker than 2mm. Sprinkle with the pink peppercorns. Bake for eight to ten minutes or until golden on top. Remove and allow to settle for a few seconds.
With a sharp knife, cut the dough into six 5x8cm rectangles. Pick a 5cm-diameter cylindrical-shaped object. Roll the hot *tuile* around it, sealing one end over the other. Hold until it has cooled and hardened. Carefully remove the tuile from the cylinder and store in airtight container until just before using. Repeat until you have six tuile cylinders.

The tuiles must be warm for molding. If they have hardened a little when cooling, reheat in the oven for a few seconds, then mold quickly.

Blackberry coulis

Gently rinse the blackberries and pat them dry. Set six aside for garnish. In a blender purée the rest with the sugar until obtaining a thick juice. Strain and cook for five minutes over low heat. Remove from heat; cool.

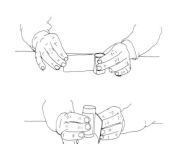

Presentation

Place a tuile cylinder in the center of each plate. Fill carefully with curuba ice cream. Garnish with a lemongrass leaf and a halved blackberry; drizzle with a ribbon of blackberry coulis.

Kyoto

Chocolate rolls with rice cream, wasabi and assorted fruit purées

4 servings

Ingredients

Rice and wasabi cream
- 1 ¹/₂ cups milk
- 1 large ginger root, sliced
- 1 cup coconut milk,
  see Appendix, page 179
- 1 cup white rice
- ¹/₂ cup light syrup,
  see Appendix, page 181
- 1 teaspoon powdered *wasabi*

Chocolate rolls
- 1 cup chocolate temper,
  see Appendix, page 178

Fruit
- ¹/₄ cup *uchuvas*
- ¹/₄ cup *agrás*
- 1 tablespoon sugar
- ¹/₄ cup strawberries
- 4 sprigs of mint

Special equipment
- measuring cup
- 3cm wide *rodoid* plastic, to yield 12
10cm strips
- adhesive tape
- waxed paper

Preparation

Rice and wasabi cream

In a heavy-duty saucepan, heat the milk with the ginger root slices until boiling; remove from heat. Allow to infuse for 15 minutes. Strain, discarding ginger. Reheat the milk with the coconut milk. Add the rice and cook covered over low heat until *al dente,* about 12 minutes. Remove from heat; allow to settle. In a blender, purée the rice with the light syrup. Drain and add the powdered wasabi. Cover with plastic wrap; store in the refrigerator until serving.

Chocolate rolls

Prepare the chocolate following the process in the Appendix. Cut 3cm-wide rodoid plastic into twelve 10cm-long strips. Spread the chocolate temper over each strip, leaving half a centimeter margin at one end. Roll into a cylinder with the chocolate on the inside. Seal the roll with the half centimeter margin; secure with a strip of adhesive tape. Place the rolls on a sheet pan lined with waxed paper.

Chill in the refrigerator until the chocolate hardens. Remove the rolls from refrigerator. Make a cone of waxed paper, fill with chocolate temper. Using the cone as a pastry bag, squeeze a little of the chocolate temper into the rolls to seal the bottom. Refrigerate again, uncovered, until hardened.

Fruit

Wash the fruit well. Reserve two uchuvas and 12 agrás berries for garnish. To prepare the uchuva, purée the remaining uchuvas in the blender until smooth. Cover and store in the refrigerator.
To prepare the agrás, purée the remaining agrás in the blender with the sugar and a tablespoon of water. Cover and store in the refrigerator. To prepare the strawberries, purée all the strawberries in the blender. Cover; store in the refrigerator.

Assembly

Remove the 12 chocolate rolls from the refrigerator and carefully peel off the plastic. With each of the three purées fill four chocolate rolls half a centimeter high with the fruit compotes. Make four of each flavor. Top the rest of each roll with the rice and wasabi cream.

Presentation

Garnish the rolls with halved uchuvas, agrás berries, and mint sprigs. Place three on each plate.

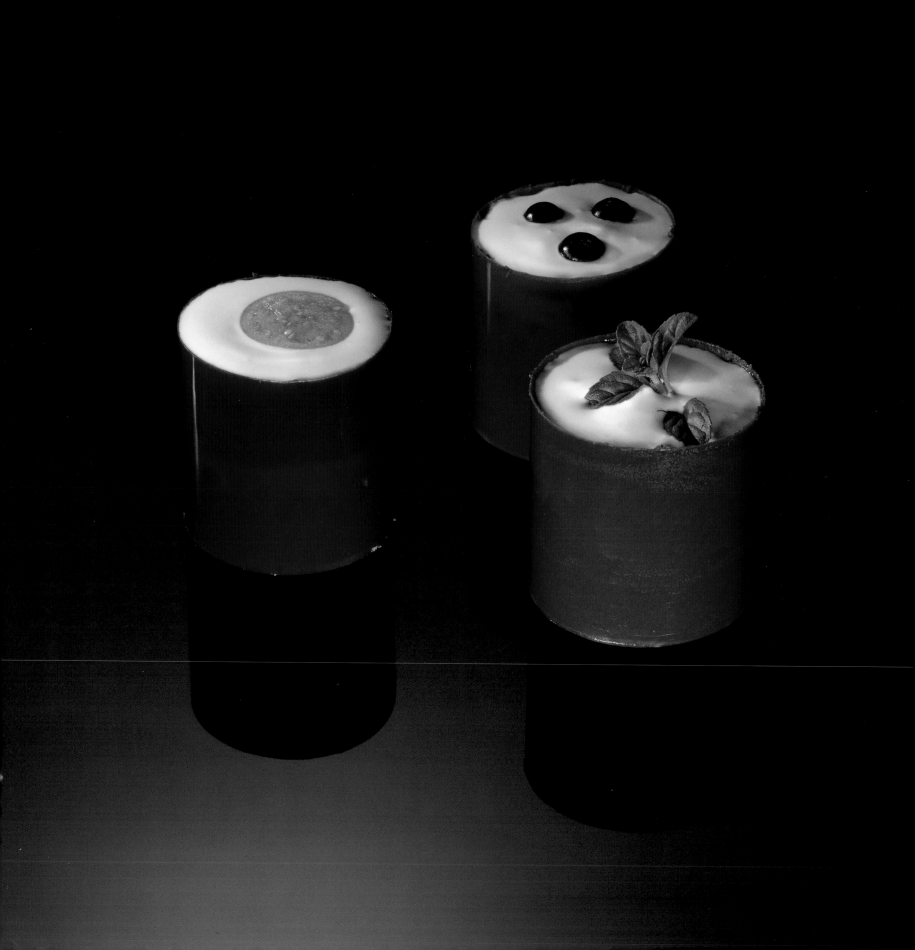

Taj Mahal

Millefeuille of crispy apples, iced saffron cream and caramel

4 servings

Ingredients

Saffron cream
- ½ leaf of gelatin
- ⅛ cup sugar
- 3 egg yolks
- 1 cup heavy cream
- 7 saffron strands

Crispy apples
- 2 green apples, rinsed
- 2 cups light syrup, see Appendix, page 181

Saffron caramel
- syrup used to cook the apples
- 8 saffron strands

Garnish
- 4 mint sprigs

Special equipment
- measuring cup
- mandoline
- *silpat* sheet or medium-sized baking sheet pan
- waxed paper

Preparation

Saffron cream

Soak the gelatin in iced water until softened.

In a bowl, beat the sugar with the egg yolks until pale and creamy. Place in bain-marie and beat the sugar and egg yolks constantly until the mixture doubles in volume. Do not allow the temperature of the water bath to exceed 120°F/50°C. The mixture must be heated only slightly. Remove from heat.
Simmer the cream with the saffron; do not let it boil. Remove from heat. Drain the gelatin and dissolve it in a little warm cream, pour this over the remaining cream. Mix well. Fold the mixture into the beaten egg yolks. Chill thoroughly. Beat again to lighten. Store in refrigerator.

Crispy apples

Preheat the oven to 200°F/94°C.
Wash the apples. With a mandoline, slice the apples very thin; you will need at least 20 slices. Put in the syrup and cook over low heat until the apple is transparent. Remove from heat. With tongs, remove the apple slices, shaking off excess syrup, and arrange on a silpat sheet or sheet pan lined with waxed paper. Reserve the syrup. Bake until dry and golden. Remove from oven and spread on creased aluminium foil to give the slices turn wavy. After cooling, store in an airtight container to retain crispiness.

Saffron caramel

Heat the syrup used to cook the apples. Add the saffron strands, boil until slightly thickened.

Presentation

In the center of each plate, place a slice of crispy apple and cover with saffron cream. Build four layers, alternating saffron cream with apple slices; finish with slice of crispy apple. Drizzle each plate with saffron caramel; garnish with a sprig of mint.

Macondo

Macadamia nut tacos with guava flowers and guacamole

6 servings

Ingredients

Tacos
- ⅓ cup *macadamia* nuts, ground
- ⅓ cup sugar
- ¼ cup flour
- ¼ cup melted butter
- 2 small eggs
- 1 teaspoon vanilla extract

Avocado cream
- 2 small ripe avocados
- ⅓ cup sugar
- juice of ½ a lemon

Guava flowers
- 6 slightly unripe guavas, rinsed
- ¼ cup light syrup,
  see Appendix, page 181

Cassis coulis
- 1 cup *crème de cassis*

Special equipment
- measuring cup
- 1 *silpat* sheet
- 30x40cm sheet pan
- circular biscuit cutter 15cm in diameter
- pastry bag
- mandoline

Preparation

Tacos
Mix the nuts with the sugar and flour. Add the melted butter, eggs and vanilla extract. With an electrical mixer whip all ingredients thoroughly. Chill for about half an hour.

Preheat the oven to 300°F/150°C. Remove the batter from the refrigerator. With a flexible metal spatula, spread the batter over a silpat sheet or over a 30x40 greased and floured sheet pan, in an even layer not thicker than 2mm. Bake for ten minutes or until golden. Select a 15cm biscuit cutter. Remove the tuiles from the oven. With the biscuit cutter, work quickly to stamp out six rounds. Pick a cylindrical object 6cm in diameter. Still working quickly, shape the hot tuiles into tacos, wraping them around the cylinder and holding each taco together until it cools and hardens. Carefully detach from cylinder. Keep the tacos in an airtight container.

The tuiles must be warm for molding. If they have hardened a little when cooling, reheat in the oven for a few seconds, then mold quickly.

Avocado cream
Prepare the avocado cream just before serving to avoid browning. Peel the avocados and remove pits. In the blender process the pulp with the sugar and lemon until smooth.

Guava flowers
Cut off the two guava ends and, with a mandoline, cut into very thin slices. Choose the nicest slices, and dip them in the cold syrup. Set a flower on each plate and the taco beside it.

Cassis coulis
Cook the crème de cassis over medium heat until reduced to a light syrup.

Presentation
Fit a pastry bag with a smooth-tip and fill each taco with the avocado cream. Garnish with the cassis coulis on the side or spooned onto the taco.

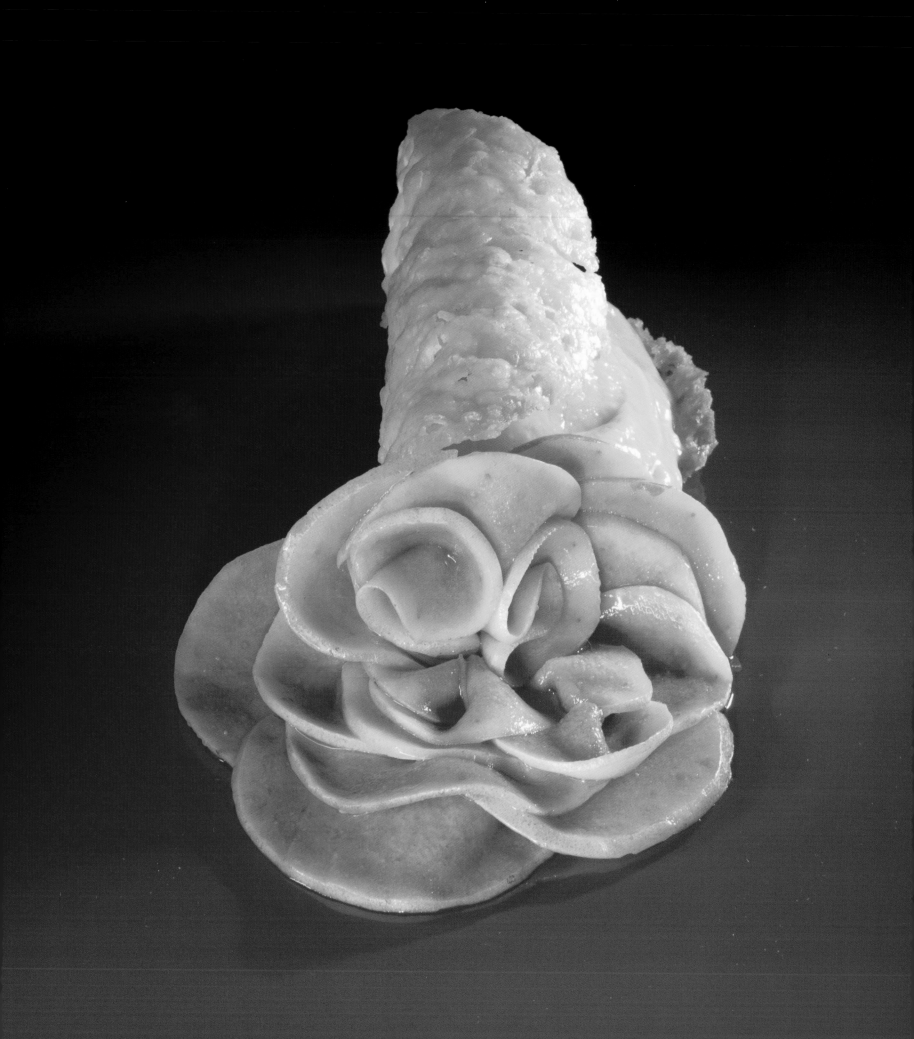

Katmandu

Chocolate and curry cake with coconut ice cream

6 servings

Ingredientes

Chocolate génoise
- see Appendix, page 177

Curry cream
- 2 leaves of gelatin
- 3 cups heavy cream
- 1 tablespoon *curry* powder, plus a few pinches reserved for garnish
- 8 egg yolks
- ½ cup sugar

Coconut ice cream
- 2 cups coconut milk, see Appendix, page 179
- 5 egg yolks
- ¾ cup sugar
- 1 cup heavy cream
- 1 cup grated coconut

Chocolate tablets
- 1 cup chocolate temper to yield 12 tablets, see Appendix, page 178

Chocolate glaze
- see Appendix, page 178

Special equipment
- measuring cup
- ice cream maker
- two 40x30cm rectangular baking molds or 2 *silpat* sheets
- 4cm wide *rodoid* plastic strips

Preparation

Chocolate génoise

Prepare the chocolate *génoise* following the recipe in the Appendix.

Curry cream

Soak the gelatin in iced water until softened.

Mix the cream with the curry powder and cook over medium heat for five minutes, taking care to avoid boiling. Remove from heat; allow to settle. In a separate bowl, beat the egg yolks with the sugar until pale and creamy. Slowly whisk the hot cream onto the beaten eggs. Transfer the mixture to a heavy-duty saucepan and cook over low heat. Stir constantly with a wooden spoon until the foam disappears from the surface and the mixture coats the back of the spoon. Take care not to let the mixture boil. Remove from heat and immediately strain into a bowl set over an ice bath. Add the drained gelatin and stir until gelatin is completely dissolved. Before using, beat with an electric mixer until aerated and light.

Coconut ice cream

Heat the coconut milk. In a bowl, beat the egg yolks with the sugar until pale and creamy. Add half the cream; mix well. Slowly whisk the hot coconut milk into the beaten egg yolks and cream. Transfer to a heavy-duty saucepan and cook over low heat. Stir constantly with a wooden spoon, without letting boil, until the foam disappears from the surface and the mixture coats the back of the spoon. Remove from heat and strain into a bowl set over an ice bath. Add the rest of the cream and the grated coconut; mix well. Allow to settle and chill completely. Pour into an ice cream machine and proceed according to the manufacturer's instructions. Chill until serving.

Chocolate tablets

Prepare 12 tablets following the recipe in the Appendix.

Chocolate glaze

Prepare the chocolate glaze following the recipe in the Appendix.

Cake assembly

Cut the génoise in five equal rectangles. With a flexible metal spatula, spread a thin, even layer of curry cream over four of them. Stack the four rectangles one on top of the other and finish with the one without cream. Frost with chocolate glaze and refrigerate until hardened. Before serving, remove the cake from refrigerator and cut a thin slice off each side to eliminate the slices with excess glaze. Slice into six equal portions.

Presentation

Place each cake slice in the center of each plate. Garnish with the chocolate tablets set on a diagonal, and accompany with a scoop of coconut ice cream very lightly sprinkled with curry powder.

Kiev

Chocolate and beet spirals

6 servings

Ingredients

Beet and chocolate cream

- 1 beet
- 1 teaspoon wine vinegar
- 1 teaspoon sugar
- pinch of salt
- $1/8$ cup heavy cream
- $3^1/2$ oz dark chocolate, finely chopped

Chocolate sauce

- $1/2$ cup sugar
- $1/4$ cup wine vinegar
- $1/4$ cup balsamic vinegar
- 2 tablespoons unsweetened cocoa powder

Beet sauce

- 1 portion of beet purée (see beet and chocolate cream preparation, above)
- $1/4$ cup water
- 1 teaspoon lemon juice
- 1 tablespoon sugar

Special equipment

- kitchen scales
- measuring cup
- mandoline
- 2 squeeze bottles

Preparation

Beet and chocolate cream

Simmer the beet in a little water with vinegar, sugar, and salt, until tender. Remove from heat, cool, peel and with a mandoline, cut half the beet in very thin slices; 1mm if possible. Cover with plastic wrap and chill. Purée the remaining beet half in the blender. Divide this purée in two equal portions. Heat the cream, without letting it boil, and pour it over the chocolate. Stir with a wooden spoon until the chocolate has completely melted. If the hot cream fails to melt all the chocolate, gently warm the mixture in bain-marie. Add one portion of beet purée, mix well, and chill, covered. Reserve the other portion of beet purée for the sauce.

Chocolate sauce

In a nonreactive saucepan, over medium heat, completely dissolve the sugar in the two vinegars. Raise the heat and cook until the mixture reduces and acquires the texture of light caramel. With a wooden spoon, stir the cocoa into the mixture, mixing thoroughly. Remove from heat and allow to settle.

Beet sauce

In a saucepan, combine the remaining beet purée, water, lemon juice and sugar. Cook over medium heat for two minutes. Remove from heat and pass through a fine sieve or cheesecloth.

Presentation

Transfer the chocolate sauce and the beet sauce into separate squeeze bottles. Starting in the center of each plate, draw two spirals: one of chocolate, the other of beet sauce. Arrange 12 cones with the beet slices and top with beet and chocolate cream. Place two on each plate.

Surinam

Chocolate and mamoncillo cake

8 servings

Ingredients

Chocolate cake

- 1 cup water
- 1³/₄ oz unsweetened cocoa powder
- 1 cup sifted flour
- 1 tablespoon baking powder
- pinch of baking soda
- 1 teaspoon salt
- 4³/₈ oz butter
- 1 cup sugar
- 3 eggs

Mamoncillo purée

- 2⁵/₈ oz Italian meringue, see Appendix, page 180
- 35 oz *mamoncillos*

Chocolate glaze

- 17 oz semisweet chocolate, finely chopped
- 2¹/₂ cups heavy cream
- 1¹/₃ cups corn syrup

Mamoncillo coulis

- 17 oz mamoncillos
- 2 cups milk
- 3 egg yolks
- ¹/₂ cup sugar

Special equipment

- kitchen scales
- measuring cup
- 20cm round cake pan
- long serrated pan knife

Preparation

Chocolate cake

Preheat the oven to 350°F/175°C. Grease and lightly flour the cake pan. Boil the water and slowly whisk in the cocoa. Mix well and remove from heat. Sift the flour with the baking powder, baking soda and salt.

In a deep bowl, beat the butter until creamy. Add the water and cocoa in three passes, alternating with the dry, sifted ingredients. Add the eggs one by one and beat until well mixed. Pour mixture into the pan and bake for 45 minutes or until a cake tester comes out clean. Cool for 15 minutes before unmolding. Cool completely before assembling the cake.

Mamoncillo purée

Prepare the Italian meringue following the recipe in Appendix, page 180. Peel the mamoncillos. Scrape the pulp off with a knife; discard the pits. Fold the pulp into the meringue.

Chocolate glaze

In a saucepan, heat the cream with the corn syrup. Pour the hot cream over the chocolate and mix until the chocolate melts completely and the mixture is smooth. If the hot cream fails to melt all the chocolate, warm up in bain-marie. Transfer the glaze to a clean bowl, cover with plastic wrap and reserve at room temperature.

Mamoncillo coulis

Peel the mamoncillos. Remove the pulp by scraping with a knife; discard the pits. Boil the milk with the pulp. In a separate bowl, beat the egg yolks with the sugar until pale and creamy. Slowly pour the hot milk over the beaten yolks and stir. Transfer the mixture to a heavy-duty saucepan and cook over low heat. Stir constantly with a wooden spoon, taking care not to boil, until the foam disappears from the surface and the mixture coats the back of the spoon. Pour into a bowl set over an ice bath; cool. Cover with plastic wrap and chill.

Assembly

With a long serrated knife, cut the cake in half horizontally. Cover one half with mamoncillo purée, spreading it evenly until forming a layer 1cm thick. Place the other cake round on top. Pour the chocolate glaze over the top of the cake and frost evenly with a flexible metal spatula. With a smaller spatula, trace furrows over the glaze. Store cake in refrigerator.

Presentation

Cut the cake in eight slices. Place one in the center of each plate. Garnish with a sliced-open mamoncillo and spoon some mamoncillo coulis on the side.

Fennel parfait with peach granité

8 servings

Ingredients

Fennel parfait
- 1 1/2 gelatin leaves
- 2 tablespoons water
- ¹/₄ cup sugar
- 1 teaspoon lemon juice
- 2 egg yolks
- 1 egg
- ¹/₂ cup milk
- 3¹/₂ oz fresh fennel, chopped
- 1 1/2 tablespoons pastis
- ¹/₂ cup heavy cream, well chilled

Peach granité
- 3 peaches
- ¹/₂ cup water

Special equipment
- kitchen scales
- measuring cup
- candy thermometer
- 2 metal rings, 11cm in diameter and 3¹/₃cm deep

Preparation

Fennel parfait
Soak the gelatin in iced water until softened.

In a heavy-duty saucepan, boil the water, sugar, and lemon juice. With a wet pastry brush, clean the inner edges of the pan to prevent the sugar from crystallizing. Cook until the syrup reaches 250°F/121°C, or the hard ball stage.

Beat the yolks with the egg. Beating constantly, add the syrup in a thin trickle. Continue beating until the mixture cools completely. Boil the milk with the fennel for two minutes. Remove from heat, cool for ten minutes. Purée in the blender, strain, and mix with the beaten egg yolks.

Heat the pastis, add the drained gelatin and dissolve. Mix thoroughly with the batter.

With an electric mixer, beat the cold cream until it forms soft peaks and gently fold in the rest of the preparation. To make a bottom for the metal rings, place each ring on a piece of plastic wrap and press the overlapping edges to the outer surface. Pour the *parfait* into the rings, and smooth down the surface with the back of a spoon or a small offset spatula. Cover with aluminium foil and cool for at least an hour. A quarter of an hour before serving, put rings in the refrigerator to improve texture upon serving.

Peach granité
Peel the peaches and remove the pits. Purée the pulp with the water in the blender. Strain and chill for at least two hours. Store in the freezer until serving.

Presentation
Remove the parfaits from refrigerator, detach the plastic and slip them out on a plate. With a knife, cut each in four and divide the quarters into three triangular pieces.

Arrange three parfait triangles on each plate, imitating the form of a star. Remove the peach ice from the freezer, scraping with a spoon for the granité. Garnish the plate with three tablespoons of granité between the triangles and serve immediately.

Havana

Sautéed and caramelized baby bananas with nutmeg cream

4 servings

Ingredients

Nutmeg cream

- ½ leaf of gelatin
- ⅛ cup sugar
- 3 egg yolks
- 1 cup heavy cream
- ½ teaspoon nutmeg

Bananas

- 1 oz butter
- 1 teaspoon corn syrup
- ½ cup sugar
- 8 baby bananas, peeled
- ½ cup orange juice

Special equipment

- kitchen scales
- measuring cup

Preparation

Nutmeg cream

Soak the gelatin in iced water until softened.

In a heavy-duty saucepan, mix the sugar with the egg yolks. Place in bain-marie. Do not allow temperature of water to exceed 120F°/50°C. Beat constantly until the mixture doubles in volume. It must warm only slightly. Remove from heat. In a separate pan, cook the cream with the nutmeg, without letting it boil. Remove from heat. Drain the gelatin and dissolve in two tablespoons of the hot cream. Pour over the remaining cream; mix well. Slowly add the mixture to the beaten egg yolks, stirring constantly. Chill thoroughly. Just before serving, beat with an electric mixer until light and airy.

Bananas

In a frying pan, over medium heat, combine the butter, corn syrup and sugar. When they start to bubble, add the bananas. Shake the frying pan occasionally so the bananas caramelize evenly. During the caramelization process, gradually add the orange juice. When the bananas are golden, remove from heat and serve immediately.

Presentation

Place two bananas in the center of each plate, and pour a little caramel over them. With a teaspoon scoop out little *quenelle*-shaped ovals of nutmet cream. Garnish with the quenelles of nutmeg cream and a sprig of mint.

Cheesecake champignon with ginger and raspberries

6 servings

Ingredients

Cheesecake

- 3 cups cream cheese
- 1 cup sugar
- 3 egg yolks
- 3/4 cup sour cream
- 1 tablespoon powdered ginger
- 3 egg whites

Garnish

- 1/2 cup chocolate sauce, see Appendix, page 178
- 1 cup chocolate sprinkles
- 1 1/2 cups raspberries
- 1/2 cup Japanese pink ginger slices
- 1 cup raspberry coulis, see Appendix, page 182

Special equipment

- 1 measuring cup
- 6 round baking pans, 6cm in diameter
- pastry brush
- waxed paper

Preparation

Cheesecake

Preheat the oven to 350F°/175°C.
Line the baking pans with waxed paper.
With an electric or manual beater, beat the cream cheese with the sugar, then add the egg yolks, sour cream and ginger. Beat until smooth.
Separately, beat the egg whites until foamy and pour over the cheese mixture. Fold gently to combine.
Pour cheesecake batter to each pan; spread evenly. Leave a 1 cm space below the edge. Bake for 45 to 60 minutes, until firm. Turn off the oven, open the door and allow to cool for one hour before removing the pans.

Garnish

Unmold the cheescakes, without disturbing the mushroom top formed by the rising dough. With a knife, cut the lower part, maintaining the circular shape to imitate a mushroom stalk. With a brush, dab the mushrom heads with the chocolate sauce. Then sprinkle liberally with chocolate sprinkles.

Presentation

Place a cheesecake champignon on each plate. Garnish by scattering raspberries and pink ginger slices on the side. Pour a little raspberry coulis on top.

People and individuals have their own identity. They are distinguished by the culture that has made them recognizable to the eyes of the world, through the peculiarities of their behaviour and customs, but also throught the use they have made of products that nature has given them. When we hear the word *curry,* we inevitably think of India or Pakistan, just as Mexico comes to mind at the mention of a mixture of chocolate and hot peppers. We think of France, when wild mushrooms appear, of peasant wisdom that distinguishes between venomous and edible. We think of Alsace or Germany at the sight of *choucroute* and of Arab and Mediterranean countries when eggplant or chickpeas, garlic and olives are present in the kitchen.

Albeit originally from China, would it be possible to dissociate spaghetti from Italy, which displays pasta to the world as a national symbol? And raw fish, could it bring to mind any other country than Japan? One can say that the memory of taste always refers to a place of origin, to a precise geography or culture which, in the case of the following dessert suggestions, has been called ethnic. Where do the potato, cassava, cacao, tapioca, which spread throughout the world, originally come from? And where do pineapple, the tropical product *par excellence*, just as the coconut, mango, and passion fruit originate? There is a touch of exotism in the very resonance of these words.

In this play of creation, as all creation is, in principle, imagination at play, I have tried to restore each dessert to an identity, a country, and a culture. Whoever savours these desserts will "travel" to the locations that gave origin to their distinct taste. South America, China, Japan, Thailand, France, Italy or United States of America — what matters is not the destination of the "journey" but the evocation by each flavor of the place where it emerged. A particular ingredient, or the manner of preparing it, gives birth to a new and original product. But originality does not prevent the memory of taste to make its "journey to the seed bed" or to remote origins.

Ogaki

Fruit sushi with lychee rice

4 servings

Ingredients

Lychee rice
- 1 cup milk
- 1 cup coconut milk, see Appendix, page 179
- 1 cup white rice
- 3 tablespoons sugar
- 2 cups *lychees* in syrup

Fruit
- 8 strawberries, rinsed
- 1 red mango, rinsed and peeled
- 2 kiwis, rinsed and peeled
- 2 *pitahayas*

Special equipment
- measuring cup
- mandoline
- waxed paper

Preparation

Lychee rice
Heat the milk with coconut milk until boiling; remove from heat. Stir in the rice and cook, covered, over low heat until *al dente*. Add the sugar, mix well and cook a few minutes longer. Remove from heat and allow to cool.

Cover the rice with plastic wrap and store in the refrigerator.

Drain the lychees and purée in the blender with a tablespoon of their syrup. When the rice is cool, mix very gently with the lychee purée. Chill until serving.

Fruit
Slice the fruit very thinly with a mandoline.

Sushi assembly
Place a sheet of waxed paper on the working table. With a spoon, spread the rice over it. Using the paper as a guide, roll the rice into a long cylinder. Cut 16 equal rolls.

Presentation
On each plate, place four rice rolls. Cover each with slices of each fruit, pressing the slices onto the roll.

Hawaii

Macadamia nougat with orange coulis

8 servings

Ingredients

Nougat

- ¾ cup water
- 3 cups sugar
- ½ cup corn syrup
- ¾ cup honey
- 4 egg whites
- ⅜ cup confectioners' sugar
- 1 lb 2 oz *macadamia* nuts
- ¼ cup grated orange rind
- corn starch for sprinkling
- *oblea* sheets

Angel hair

- see Appendix, page 175

Orange coulis

- 1 cup orange juice
- 1 cup sugar
- 2 tablespoons port
- 1 tablespoon *Grand Marnier*
- 1 tablespoon corn starch

Special equipment

- kitchen scales
- measuring cup
- 2 candy thermometers
- electric beater
- 5cm biscuit cutter,

Preparation

Nougat

For best results, keep a close watch on the temperatures of both the syrup and the honey.

In a heavy-duty saucepan, mix the water, sugar and corn syrup. Cook over medium heat, controlling temperature with a candy thermometer and clean the inner rim of the pan with a wet pastry brush. When the syrup reaches 265°F/130°C, heat the honey in another pan, to 250°F/121°C. Meanwhile, with an electric mixer in a separate bowl, beat the egg whites until foamy and gradually add the sugar to make a meringue. Beating constantly, add the heated honey. Then add the syrup, which should then have reached 300°F/150°C. Continue beating until the mixture has completely cooled. Add the macadamia nuts and grated orange rind; stir to spread around evenly. Pour the nougat onto it. Sprinkle the nougat with a little more corn starch. With a rolling pin, spread the nougat between sheets of waxed paper rolling until obtaining an even thickness of 1cm Place in a sheet pan and allow to dry for several hours. With the biscuit cuter, stamp 24 nougat rounds. Cut the oblea sheets in the same shape and size, and stick to both sides of the nougat.

Angel hair

Prepare angel hair following the recipe in the Appendix.

Orange coulis

On a heavy-duty saucepan, mix the orange juice with the sugar, port, and Grand Marnier. Cook over medium heat until reduced by half. Add the corn starch and stir until slightly thick. Remove from heat, strain, and cool.

Presentation

Pile three nougat rounds on each plate, garnish with angel hair and drizzle with orange coulis.

Bangkok

Coconut rice with lychees and pistachios

8 servings

Ingredients

Coconut rice
- 1 cup milk
- 1 cup coconut milk, see Appendix, page 179
- 1 cup rice
- 3 tablespoons sugar

Garnish
- 24 lychees in syrup
- $\frac{1}{2}$ cup ground pistachios

Special equipment
- measuring cup

Preparation

Coconut rice

Heat the milk with coconut milk until boiling; remove from heat. Stir in the rice, and cook, covered, over low heat until *al dente.* Add the sugar, mix well and cook a few minutes longer. Remove from heat and cool.

Cover the rice with plastic wrap and chill until serving.

Presentation

In a cup, glass or ramekin, alternate layers of coconut rice and ground pistachios. Garnish with three lychees on each plate.

Hong Kong

Tapioca pudding with coffee

8 servings

Ingredients

Tapioca pudding
- 1 cup brewed black coffee
- 2 tablespoons *Bailey's Irish Cream*
- 1 cup *tapioca*
- 2 cups milk
- 1 tablespoon instant coffee
- 3 eggs
- 2 egg yolks
- $\frac{1}{2}$ cup sugar

Coffee tuiles
- see Appendix, page 179

Vanilla génoise
- see Appendix, page 184
- 4 cups Bailey's Irish Cream
- $\frac{1}{4}$ cup milk

Coffee sauce
- 1 cup milk
- 1 tablespoon instant coffee
- 2 egg yolks
- $\frac{1}{3}$ cup sugar
- 2 tablespoons Bailey's Irish Cream

Garnish
- 6 cherries, pitted

Special equipment
- kitchen scales
- measuring cup
- 4 metal rings, 10cm in diameter and 2.5cm deep
- sheet of *silpat* or waxed paper
- pastry brush

Preparation

Tapioca pudding

Heat the coffee with the Bailey's Irish Cream, pour over the tapioca and allow to soak for at least two hours. In another saucepan, heat the milk with the instant coffee. In a separate bowl, beat the eggs, egg yolks and sugar until pale and creamy. Slowly whisk the hot milk into the beaten eggs. Transfer to a heavy-duty saucepan and cook over low heat. Stir constantly with a wooden spoon, without letting boil, until the foam disappears from the surface and the mixture coats the back of the spoon. Remove from heat and strain in a bowl set over an ice bath. Cool and chill thoroughly in the refrigerator.

Coffee tuiles

Prepare the coffee *tuiles* following the recipe in the Appendix.

Vanilla génoise

Prepare the vanilla *génoise* following the recipe in the Appendix.
Mix the milk with Bailey's Irish Cream, to moisten the génoise later.

Coffee sauce

Heat the milk with the instant coffee until boiling; remove from heat. In a separate bowl, beat the egg yolks with the sugar until pale and creamy. Slowly whisk the hot milk into the beaten egg yolks. Transfer to a heavy-duty saucepan and cook over low heat. Stir constantly with a wooden spoon, without letting boil, until the foam disappears from the surface and the mixture coats the back of the spoon. Strain into a bowl set over an ice bath and cool.

Assembly

Preheat the oven to 300°F/150°C. Arrange the metal rings on a sheet pan lined with waxed paper or a silpat sheet Cut six circles of génoise the size of the rings and brush with the milk and Bailey's Irish Cream mixture reserved for this purpose. Place a round of génoise at the bottom of each ring. Pour the coffee and tapioca pudding mixture up to half a centimeter below the rim of the rings and place in the oven. After 30 minutes, remove and fill to the brim with a layer of the soaked tapioca. Pour in a little more coffee and tapioca pudding mixture and put in the oven again for 20 minutes. Remove and allow to cool for five minutes before unmolding.

Presentation

Pour a little coffee sauce on each plate and place a pudding on top. Garnish with a tuile and a cherry.

Tolima

Passionfruit jelly tamale stuffed with coconut

4 servings

Ingredients

Passionfruit jelly
- 4 leaves of gelatin
- 3 $^1/_3$ cups passionfruit juice
- 5 tablespoons sugar, or more, to taste depending on juice acidity

Coconut stuffing
- $^7/_8$ oz butter
- 2 tablespoons brown sugar
- $^1/_2$ cup grated *panela*
- 1 cup grated coconut
- $^1/_2$ cup coconut milk, see Appendix, page 179

Garnish
- 4 thin strips of banana leaf

Special equipment
- kitchen scales
- measuring cup
- 25cm square baking pan
- pastry plastic
- pastry bag
- adhesive tape

Preparation

Passionfruit jelly

Soak the gelatin in iced water until softened.

Mix the passionfruit juice with the sugar, reserving a few tablespoons of juice to dissolve the gelatin. Add the gelatin mixture to the rest of the juice and stir well. Line the baking pan with two rectangular sheets of plastic. Transfer the mixture to the pan, pouring a layer that's 1 cm deep. Reserve the remaining passionfruit mixure to seal the rolls. Chill until firm.

Coconut stuffing

Melt the butter with the brown sugar and panela. Cook over medium heat until it begins to caramelize. Add the coconut and coconut milk. Stir well with a wooden spoon and cook until the liquid evaporates. Remove from heat and cool.

Tamale assembly

Once the passionfruit jelly is quite firm, cut into two rectangles the same size as the plastic sheets used as bottom, unmold, and transfer to a working surface. Fill a pastry bag without the nozzle with the cooled coconut stuffing. Hold one of the jelly rectangles in your hand lengthwise, with its plastic base, and pipe the coconut stuffing over it. Fold into a roll and seal with three strips of adhesive tape at the ends and middle. Pour a little jelly over the seam to seal. Repeat this process with the other rectangle. Cool until *rolls* are well sealed.

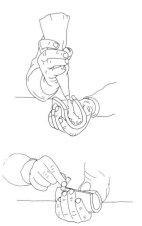

Presentation

Remove the *tamales* from refrigerator. Carefully detach the adhesive tape and plastic without touching the roll.

Cut each roll into two equal parts. Place one on each plate and garnish with a thin strip of banana leaf. Serve immediately.

Ottawa

Crumbed cheesecake fingers with tree tomato coulis

8 servings

Ingredients

Cheesecake
- 3 cups cream cheese
- 1 cup sugar
- 3 egg yolks
- ³⁄₄ cup sour cream
- 1 tablespoon vanilla extract
- 3 egg whites

Crumbing
- 2 beaten eggs
- 1 cup *petit-beurre* crumbs
- 2 cups vegetable oil

Tree tomato coulis
- 4 *tree tomatoes*
- honey according to taste

Special equipment
- measuring cup
- 30x40cm cake pan
- waxed paper

Preparation

Cheesecake

Preheat the oven to 350°F/175°C.
Line the baking sheet with waxed paper.
With an electric mixer beat the cream
cheese with the sugar, add the egg yolks,
sour cream and vanilla extract. Beat until
batter is smooth. Beat the egg whites
until foamy and pour carefully over the
cheese mixture, folding with a spatula.
Pour the cheesecake batter into the cake
pan and spread evenly to 1cm below the
rim. Bake for one hour and 15 minutes.
Turn off the oven, open the door, and
allow the cheesecake to settle for one
hour before removing from oven.
Unmold, cool thoroughly, and cut little
fingers 5cm long and 1cm wide.

Tree tomato coulis

Peel the tree tomatoes, purée thoroughly
in the blender, and strain. Add honey to
taste, mix well, and cook over low heat
for five minutes. Cool.

Crumbing

Dip the cheesecake fingers in the
beaten eggs, shaking off excess egg,
and dredge in the petit-beurre crumbs.
Fry in hot vegetable oil until evenly
golden. Drain on paper towels. Don't let
the fried cheesecake sit before serving.

Presentation

Place five little fingers on each plate and
drizzle with droplets of tree tomato
coulis.

Barlovento

Frozen pineapple in coconut and rum sauce

8 servings

Ingredients

Pineapple
- 1 small pineapple
- 8 lemongrass stalks

Coconut and rum sauce
- 2 cups coconut milk, see Appendix, page 179
- $1/3$ cup rum
- 8 tablespoons sugar

Special equipment
- measuring cup
- apple corer
- 8 wooden skewers

Preparation

Pineapple
Peel the pineapple well, taking care to remove the "eyes." With an apple corer, cut eight cylinders. Slice off the ends to get a more attractive shape. Insert a wooden skewer in each cylinder and place in the freezer.

Coconut and rum sauce
In a bowl, combine the coconut milk, rum and sugar, mixing thoroughly. Cover with plastic wrap and refrigerate. Stir again just before serving.

Preparation
Fill eight small glasses halfway with the coconut and rum mixture. Place a cylinder of frozen pineapple in each glass, and garnish each with a lemongrass stalk.

Machu Picchu

Medley of some typical Latin American sweets

8 servings

Ingredients

Papayuela preserve
- 18 oz *papayuela*
- 4 cups water
- juice of half a lemon
- 1 cup sugar

Cocada
- 1 coconut, grated
- the reserved coconut water
- 1 1/2 cups sugar
- 2 cloves
- 1/2 lemon

Panela treacle
- 1 loaf of *panela*
- 2 cups milk
- 1 orange

Cassava ringlets
- 1 large cassava
- 2 cups light syrup, see Appendix, page 181

Special equipment
- kitchen scales
- measuring cup
- mandoline
- sheet of *silpat* or waxed paper

Preparation

Papayuela preserve

Peel the papayuelas, remove seeds, and cut into chunks. In a heavy-duty saucepan, combine the water, lemon juice and papayuela pieces and cook over low heat for 30 minutes. Add the sugar and cook for another 30 minutes, skimming as needed. Do not stir. Cool at room temperature. Strain and purée in the blender. Pour into clean glass jars, and store covered in the refrigerator.

Cocada

In a saucepan, cook the grated coconut, coconut water, one cup of the sugar and cloves over medium heat. When the syrup starts to thicken, add the rest of the sugar and the lemon juice. Cook, stirring with a wooden spoon, until the mixture darkens and thickens. The color of the *cocada* will depend on how much you let the syrup darker.
Moisten a large dinner plate or platter with water, pour the mixture over it, and cool.

Panela treacle

In a pan, cover the shredded panela in water and heat. As soon as it simmers, add interspersed trickles of milk and orange juice to clear the mixture. With a wooden spoon, discard impurities floating on the surface along with the foam, until the mixture remains totally limpid and no longer foams. Allow to boil until reaching desired thickness and remove from heat.

Cassava ringlets

Preheat the oven to 250°F/121°C. Peel the cassava. Cut 12 very thin lengthwise slices with a mandoline. Put the slices in the syrup, and cook over low heat until translucent. Remove from heat. Remove from heat. Remove the cassava slices, shaking off excess syrup, and place them on a silpat sheet or on a sheet pan lined with waxed paper. Bake until dry and golden. Remove from heat and wrap around a cylindrical object to get a loop shape, leaving one end slightly protruding. Return them to the sheet pan to cool. Once ringlets are cool, carefully remove them from sheet pan and store in an airtight container to preserve crispness.

Presentation

Place two cassava ringlets on each plate. Fill one of them with the cocada mixture. With a teaspoon, shape two *quenelles* with the papayuela preserve and the cocada and lay them on the other cassava ringlet. Drizzle with a ribbon of panela treacle.

Guadalajara

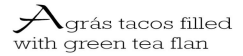grás tacos filled
with green tea flan

4 servings

Ingredients

Agrás tacos

- $2^5/_8$ oz butter
- $2^5/_8$ oz confectioners' sugar
- 3 egg whites
- $^1/_2$ cup flour
- $^1/_4$ cup *agrás,* washed

Green tea filling

- 2 cups milk
- 1 tablespoon green tea
- 3 eggs
- 2 egg yolks
- 1 cup sugar

Agrás coulis

- see Appendix, page 175

Special equipment

- kitchen scales
- measuring cup
- *silpat* sheet
- biscuit cutter, 8cm in diameter
- custard mold

Preparation

Agrás tacos

Preheat the oven to 300°F/150°C.
Cream the butter, add the sugar and,
with an electric mixer, beat until creamy.
Add the egg whites gradually, beating
constantly. At this point, the mixture
tends to separate: this is normal. Finally,
add the flour all at once and continue
beating until the batter is smooth. Chill
for at least half an hour. With a flexible
spatula, spread the batter over a silpat
sheet or a greased and floured sheet

pan until forming an even layer not
thicker than 2mm. Wash the agrás well
and crush a little with a fork. Spread the
crushed fruit over the dough and bake
for six to eight minutes, until top is
golden. Remove the sheet pan from oven
and allow to cool for a few seconds.
While the dough is still hot, stamp out at
least 12 rounds with the biscuit cutter.
Return the rounds to the oven for a few
seconds. Remove and mold around a
cylindrical object to get a taco shape.
Repeat until you have 12 tacos. Store in
an airtight container until serving. The
tacos must be warm for molding. If they
have hardened a little when cooling,
reheat in the oven for a few seconds,
then mold quickly.

Green tea filling

Heat the milk until boiling; remove from
heat. Pour over the tea, allow to infuse for
ten minutes, and strain. In a separate
bowl, beat the eggs, egg yolks, and
sugar until pale and creamy. Reheat the
milk, slowly whisk it into the beaten
eggs.

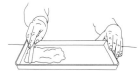

Transfer the mixture to a heavy-duty
saucepan and cook over low heat. Stir
constantly with a wooden spoon, without
letting boil, until the foam disappears
from the surface and the mixture coats
the back of the spoon. Strain to a bowl
set over an ice bath and cool.
Preheat the oven to 250°F/121°C.
Pour the mixture into a custard mold and
bake in a bain-marie for 45 minutes.
Open the door of the oven and cool for
15 minutes. Remove from oven, cool,
then chill.

Agrás coulis

Prepare the agrás coulis following the
recipe in the Appendix.

Assembly

Put the green tea filling in the blender
and process briefly; do not overblend.
With a pastry bag or a small spoon, fill
the tacos with the flan mixture.

Presentation

Place three filled tacos on each plate
and drizzle with agrás coulis.

Nagoya

Ginger flan with peaches and cellophane noodles

6 servings

Ingredients

Vanilla génoise
- 3 eggs
- $1/3$ cup sugar
- 1 teaspoon vanilla extract
- $1/2$ cup sifted flour
- $1/2$ oz butter

Ginger flan
- 2 cups milk
- 1 ginger root, sliced
- 3 eggs
- 2 egg yolks
- 1 cup sugar

Peaches
- 3 peaches
- 2 cups light syrup,
  see Appendix, page 181

Garnish
- $1/2$ cup *cellophane noodles*

Special equipment
- kitchen scales
- measuring cup
- 6 individual half-sphere shaped molds, 6cm in diameter
- sheet of *silpat*

Preparation

Vanilla génoise

With the quantities indicated, prepare the vanilla *génoise* batter following the recipe in the Appendix. On a silpat sheet or a greased and floured sheet pan, spread the batter into an even 3mm thick layer. Bake for eight to ten minutes or until the top is lightly browned. Remove from oven and cool. Cut at least 18 rounds, 6cm in diameter, making sure they are the same size as the flan molds.

Ginger flan

Heat the milk until boiling; remove from heat. Purée the ginger root in the blender with a little milk. Add the purée to the hot milk, let steep for 15 minutes and strain, discarding the ginger. In a separate bowl, beat the eggs with the egg yolks and sugar until pale and creamy. Reheat the milk, pour over the beaten eggs and stir. Transfer the mixture to a heavy-duty saucepan and cook over low heat. Stir constantly with a wooden spoon, without letting boil, until the foam disappears from the surface and the mixture coats the back of the spoon. Strain into a bowl set over an ice bath; cool.

Peaches

Prepare two cups of light syrup following the recipe in the Appendix. Peel the peaches, slice in two and remove pits. In a saucepan, cook over low heat with the light syrup for 30 minutes. Remove from heat; cool at room temperature. Remove peaches from syrup. Reserve one for the coulis and cut the four remaining halves into 1/2cm-thick slices. Process the other peach in the blender with a little syrup until obtaining a moderately thick purée.

Assembly

Preheat the oven to 250°F/121°C. With vegetable oil, grease six half-spherical 6cm molds. Line the bottom of each with the peach slices, distributing them evenly. Pour in a little of the flan mixture and place a génoise round on top. Pour more of the flan mixture and repeat the layering until filling the mold, ending with a layer of génoise. Bake for 45 minutes or until flan is firm. Remove from oven, cool for 20 minutes and chill thoroughly.

Presentation

Invert the flans onto serving plates. Garnish with cellophane noodles; drizzle with peach coulis.

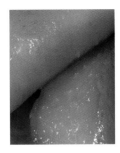

Verona

Mascarpone ravioli and pears caramelized in port

4 servings

Ingredients

Pasta
- 1 egg
- 1 teaspoon vanilla extract
- 1 vanilla bean
- ¾ cup flour
- 1 tablespoon sugar
- 1 tablespoon oil

Filling
- 2 egg yolks
- 3 tablespoons sugar
- ¼ cup *mascarpone* cheese
- ¼ cup heavy cream, well chilled
- ¼ cup ground walnuts

Pears caramelized in port
- 1 cup port
- 2 pears
- 1 tablespoon butter

Garnish
- 4 whole walnuts

Special equipment
- measuring cup
- food processor
- pasta machine
- waxed paper

Preparation

Pasta

Beat the egg with the vanilla extract. With a paring knife, slice the vanilla bean lengthwise, scrape out the seeds with the back of the knife, and add to the egg mixture. Sift the flour with the sugar and combine with the egg mixture in the food processor, pulsing until the dough just starts to hold together Do not overprocess the dough, or it will toughen. Shape the dough into a ball, wrap in plastic wrap. Chill for at least one hour.

Take the dough out of the refrigerator and place on a work surface, lightly sprinkled with flour. Roll into a rectangle. Pass the dough through a pasta machine set at maximum thickness. Fold in three, and repeat three times, reducing the thickness setting until set at minimum. Pass the dough through the minimun setting several times.

Spread the thinned sheet of dough onto the work surface and cut into 8cm squares.

Fill a pan with water, add the oil and bring to a boil. Add the pasta squares and cook for two minutes. Remove carefully; drain on clean kitchen towels. Transfer to baking sheet lined with waxed paper and cover lightly with plastic wrap.

Filling

In a bowl, beat the eggs with the sugar, and put in bain-marie. Do not let water temperature exceed 120°F/50°C. Beat constantly, with an electric or manual beater until the mixture doubles in volume. The mixture must only heat slightly. Remove from heat. Add the mascarpone cheese and beat until smooth. In a separate bowl, beat the well-chilled cream until it forms little peaks, and fold into the cheese mixture. Add the nuts and stir gently, but thoroughly.

Ravioli assembly

Put a teaspoon of filling in the center of each pasta square. Fold and pinch edges carefully to thoroughly seal in the filling; twist where the edges join so that the twisted fold remains at the center of each ravioli. Before serving, warm in a hot oven for a few seconds. Remove and serve immediately.

Pears caramelized in port

Pour the port into a frying pan and allow to reduce over medium heat for two minutes. Peel the pears, quarter them, and remove the core and seeds. Then slice each quarter in four again. Add the pears to the reduced port and cook, turning over occasionally to cook evenly. When pears are soft and lightly golden, add the butter, constantly shaking the frying-pan until completely melted. Remove from heat.

Presentation

Place 8 pear slices on each plate and drizzle with the caramel in which they were cooked. Top with two ravioli and garnish with a walnut.

Hanoi

Little rolls of julienne of celery, nectarine, apple and lemon balm

4 servings

Ingredients

Little rolls

- 2 nectarines, well rinsed
- 2 red apples, well rinsed
- juice of 1 lemon
- 2 celery stalks, well rinsed and peeled
- ½ cup light syrup, see Appendix, page 181
- 12 lemon balm leaves

Garnish

- 2 passionfruits

Special equipment

- measuring cup
- 12 fancy wooden skewers

Preparation

Little rolls

Wash the fruit and vegetables well.
Peel and slice the nectarines in a julienne.
Cut the red apples, unpeeled into a julienne, and soak in the lemon juice to avoid browning.
Slice the celery stalks into a julienne that's about 7cm-long. Boil in the light syrup for 15 minutes or until softened. Remove from heat, drain, discarding the syrup, and cool.

Presentation

On a work surface, mix the fruit and vegetables and divide them into 12 equal-sized batches. Roll each batch in a lemon balm leaf and secure each with a fancy wooden skewer.
To serve, place three rolls on each plate. Slice the passionfruit open, spoon the pulp out, and scatter it around the rolls.

Urabá

Banana cakes with plantain chips

6 servings

Ingredients

Cinnamon sauce
- 2 cups milk
- 3 egg yolks
- 1 cup sugar
- 1 teaspoon of powdered cinnamon

Banana cakes
- 2 eggs
- ¼ cup sugar
- ¼ cup sifted flour
- 3½ oz whole wheat bread cut into chunks
- 5¼ oz grated white chocolate
- 2 cups bananas, sliced

Plantain chips
- 1 large plantain
- 2 cups light syrup, see Appendix, page 181

Arequipe sauce
- ½ cup *arequipe,* see Appendix, page 176
- 2 tablespoons milk

Special equipment
- kitchen scales
- measuring cup
- 6 metal rings, 6cm in diameter and 4cm high
- sheet of *silpat* or waxed paper
- mandoline

Preparation

Cinnamon sauce

In a saucepan, heat the milk to boiling; remove from heat. In a bowl, beat the egg yolks with the sugar and cinnamon until pale and creamy. Slowly whisk the hot milk into the beaten egg yolks. Transfer the mixture to a heavy-duty saucepan and cook over low heat. Stir constantly with a wooden spoon, without letting boil, until the foam disappears from the surface and the mixture coats the back of the spoon. Strain into bowl set over an ice bath and cool.

Banana cakes

In a bowl, beat the eggs with the sugar. Add the flour and mix well. Gradually fold in the cinnamon sauce, stirring constantly. Then add the bread chunks. Cover the bowl and allow to sit for an hour and a half. Add the grated white chocolate and banana slices, stirring carefully to blend evenly.
Preheat the oven to 350°F/175°C. Grease the six metal rings. Place them on a sheet pan lined with waxed paper. Fill the rings to the brim with the mixture and bake for 30 minutes or until firm. Remove from oven and cool.

Plantain chips

Preheat the oven to 250°F/121°C. Peel the plantain. With a mandoline, cut 12 very thin lengthwise slices. Cook the bananas with syrup over low heat until translucent. Remove from heat. Remove the slices, shaking off excess syrup, and place on a sheet of silpat or in a sheet pan lined with waxed paper. Bake until dry and golden. Remove from oven and fold around a tubular object to give the shape of an open ring. Let the plantains cool and set. After cooling, detach carefully and keep in an airtight container to retain crispness.

Arequipe sauce

Prepare the arequipe following the recipe in the Appendix. In a double boiler, combine the arequipe with milk in bain-marie, cooking and stirring until it dissolves and becomes a smooth sauce. If necessary, add a little more milk.

Presentation

Unmold the cakes. Place one on each plate, pour some arequipe sauce on the side, and top with two plantain chips.

Sydney

Black figs in syrup with obleas and arequipe

4 servings

Ingredients

Black figs in syrup
- 12 black figs, rinsed and dried
- 2 cups water
- 1 cup sugar

Arequipe sauce
- ½ cup *arequipe*, see Appendix, page 176
- 2 spoonfuls of milk

Garnish
- 4 *obleas*

Special equipment
- measuring cup

Preparation

Black figs in syrup
Rub the figs' skin with a fine little sponge to remove the fuzz covering them, and make a small cross cut on top. In a heavy-duty saucepan, boil the water with the sugar. Add the black figs and cook over low heat for several hours, until figs are softened but still whole. If the syrup reduces more than desired, add hot water. You will get the best flavor if the syruyp is not too thick.
Black figs in syrup will keep in the refrigerator for up to 15 days. As they are slow to cook, it is impractical to prepare less than a dozen.

Arequipe sauce
Prepare the arequipe following the recipe in the Appendix. In a double boiler, combine the arequipe and the milk, cooking and stirring until it dissolves and becomes a smooth sauce. If necessary, add a little more milk.

Presentation
Purée four black figs in the blender with a little of their own syrup. Finely chop four black figs.
With a sharp knife, carefully cut the obleas in halves and then in triangles. In the middle of each plate, put a tablespoon of black fig purée, a tablespoon of chopped black figs, and a whole preserved fig. Stick the oblea triangles in the purée, and decorate with arequipe sauce.

Perhaps no culture exists, ancient or modern, that has failed to establish a relationship between good eating and good loving. In any book, of fact or fiction, written about love, good food will always appear. Food not only nourishes the body but also the imagination, which ignites amorous desire. There is abundant literature in this field among Western people. Bacchanalia are an expression of this, and Greek culture left us, as heritage, a rich example, divided between the dionysian and the apollonian. Between Dionysos and Bacchus, the legends establish this indissoluble bond between eating and loving.

A thirteenth-century physician from Valencia was attributed with the Catalan translation of a rare and delicious book of "erotic recipes", possibly of Arab origin: *Speculum al folgar.* Nothing escapes its anonymous author: neither hot dishes nor desserts, neither wines nor teas. Everything is included to feed the amorous imagination. This book also provides a compendium of recommendations about what one should drink and eat in each amorous circumstance, contributes to the literature of the genre in outstanding fashion. Food as aphrodisiac. That could be the title for the following series of desserts prepared for the stimulation of imagination and appetite with eclectic mixtures of aromas, flavors and textures.

To some, aphrodisiac dishes and desserts are merely suggestive, and require the aid of the imagination, without knowing with certainty if the effect is indeed the promised one. Rather than discussing this point, what matters is to know that the senses and the imagination are the main ingredients of love and of the pleasure which ensues. These desserts stimulate the imagination and the senses. More than consummation, Eros is imagination filled with desire, suggestion, arousal. The aphrodisiac dessert demands the equally aphrodisiac will of the one savouring it. Imagination completes the task initiated by smell, sight and taste.

Windsor

Kir Royal-flavored sorbets

6 servings

Ingredients

Champagne sorbet

- 2 cups champagne
- ³/₈ cups sugar

Crème de cassis sorbet

- ³/₈ cups *crème de cassis*
- 1²/₃ cups water

Garnish

- rose petals of 2 different colors

Special equipment

- measuring cup
- ice cream machine

Preparation

Champagne sorbet

In a saucepan, heat the champagne with the sugar until the sugar dissolves completely. Remove from heat, cool and chill in the refrigerator.
Put the mixture in the ice cream machine and proceed according to the manufacturer's directions. Transfer the sorbet to a deep bowl and cover with plastic wrap. Store in the freezer until serving.

Crème de cassis sorbet

In a saucepan, heat the crème de cassis with the water until boiling. Remove from heat, cool, and chill.
Put the mixture in an ice cream machine and proceed according to the manufacturer's directions. Transfer the sorbet to a deep bowl and cover with plastic wrap. Store in the freezer until serving.

Presentation

Scatter a few rose petals on each plate. Serve a scoopful of each sorbet in cups of your choice.

Andalusia

Orange and rosemary fan

4 servings

Ingredients

Oranges
- 2 oranges
- ¹/₂ cup light syrup,
  see Appendix, page 181
- 1 tablespoon fresh rosemary leaves

Rosemary tuiles
- 1 oz butter
- ¹/₄ cup confectioners' sugar
- 2 tablespoons honey
- 1 tablespoon hot water
- ¹/₃ cup sifted flour
- 1 tablespoon fresh rosemary leaves

Rosemary cream
- 1 cup heavy cream
- 3 tablespoons fresh rosemary leaves
- 2 egg yolks
- ¹/₃ cup sugar

Garnish
- 4 sprigs fresh rosemary

Special equipment
- kitchen scales
- measuring cup
- *silpat* sheet

Preparation

Oranges

To peel the oranges, cut a slice off each end and remove the peel, closely following the curve of the fruit. Slice carefully along both sides of each segment, in order to avoid the white membrane and seeds. Once you have extracted all segments, squeeze the remaining pulp over them to get all the juice.

Boil the light syrup with the rosemary leaves. Remove from heat and cool. Pour the syrup over the orange segments and marinate in the refrigerator for one hour.

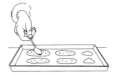

Rosemary tuiles

Over low heat, melt the butter, add the sugar and mix well. Beat until creamy. Gradually add the honey, water, and flour. Continue beating until batter is smooth. Cover with plastic wrap and chill for one hour.

Preheat the oven to 300°F/150°C. Divide the dough in small portions on a silpat sheet or on a greased and floured sheet pan. You will need at least 12 *tuiles*.

With the back of a wooden spoon, spread each portion of batter in oval form. To keep the batter from sticking to the back of the spoon, dip the spoon in cold water as needed. Leave a 2cm space between each oval. Place three rosemary leaves on each oval and bake until golden.

Rosemary cream

Heat the cream with the rosemary. Remove from heat, allow to steep for 15 minutes and strain, discarding the rosemary. In a separate bowl, beat the egg yolks with the sugar until pale and creamy. Reheat the cream, slowly whisk into the beaten eggs, and stir. Transfer the mixture to a heavy-duty saucepan and cook over low heat. Stir constantly with a wooden spoon, without letting boil, until the foam disappears from the surface and the mixture coats the back of the spoon. Strain into a bowl set over an ice bath and chill completely. Whisk with an electric beater until light and airy. Store in refrigerator.

Presentation

Place a tuile on each plate and arrange a layer of orange segments and a little rosemary cream on top. Repeat the operation, to form a fan, and finish off with a tuile. Garnish with a sprig of rosemary.

Leipzig

Apple and yogurt strudel

4 servings

Ingredients

Filling
- ¼ cup raisins
- 4 apples
- 1 tablespoon butter
- 1 tablespoon sugar
- 1 teaspoon cinnamon
- 4 tablespoons water
- ¾ cup natural yogurt

Strudel
- 4 sheets of *phyllo* dough
- ½ cup clarified butter, see Appendix, page 179
- ½ cup confectioners' sugar

Cinnamon sauce
- 2 cups milk
- 3 egg yolks
- ½ cup sugar
- 1 teaspoon powdered cinnamon

Garnish
- 8 cinnamon sticks

Special equipment
- measuring cup
- medium-sized sheet pan

Preparation

Filling

Soak the raisins in warm water until softened.

Peel and core the apples. Dice into 1 cm cubes. In a frying-pan, melt the butter, then add the sugar, cinnamon and four tablespoons of water. When the mixture starts to boil, add the apples. Cover and cook over low heat until softened and lightly golden, shaking the frying-pan occasionally to cook evenly. Pour off the liquid and add the raisins and yogurt. Mix well and cook for another five minutes. Remove from heat and cool.

Strudel

Preheat the oven to 350°F/175°C. Spread one of the phyllo sheets on the work surface. Dab with clarified butter and sprinkle with confectioners' sugar. Put another dough sheet on top and repeat. Cut into two equal rectangles. In the middle of each, pour a little filling and roll up. Pinch and twist each end 2cm from the edge, to resemble a

wrapped sweet. Reinforce twists with aluminium foil and place the strudels on a medium-sized sheet pan lined with waxed paper. Repeat the assembly with the two remaining phyllo sheets. Dab the rolls with clarified butter and sprinkle with confectioners' sugar. Bake for eight to ten minutes, taking care not to let the top layer burn.

Cinnamon sauce

In a saucepan heat the milk until boiling; remove from heat. In a separate bowl, beat the egg yolks with the sugar and cinnamon until pale and creamy. Slowly whisk the hot milk into the batter. Transfer the mixture to a heavy-duty saucepan and cook over low heat, stirring with a wooden spoon until the mixture coats the back of the spoon. Strain into a bowl set over an ice bath and cool.

Presentation

Arrange two cinnamon sticks on each plate. Set an apple strudel on top. Drizzle with cinnamon sauce; sprinkle with a little additional powdered cinnamon. Serve immediately.

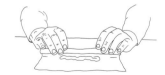

Salzburg

Chocolate textures with cherries

4 servings

Ingredients

Chocolate tablets
- 2 cups chocolate temper to yield 24 tablets, see Appendix, page 178

Chocolate and cherry ganache
- 1 cup seedless cherries, rinsed and dried
- 1 tablespoon water
- 1/4 cup heavy cream
- 5 1/8 oz semi-bitter chocolate, finely dropped

Cherry coulis
- 1 cup cherries, rinsed and dried
- 1 tablespoon water
- 1 teaspoon sugar
- 1 teaspoon lemon juice

Special equipment
- kitchen scales
- measuring cup
- *rodoid* plastic strips, 4cm-wide

Preparation

Chocolate tablets

Cut the rodoid plastic into four 24cm-long strips. Spread the chocolate temper onto them in an even 2mm thick layer, using a flexible metal spatula. Refrigerate the strips until the chocolate hardens. To get 24 tablets, score the strips every 4cm with a heated, sharp, dry knife. Wait until assembly to detach the strips.

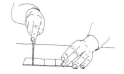

Chocolate and cherry ganache

Slice the cherries in two and remove the pits. Purée in the blender with a tablespoon of water.
Heat the cream without letting boil, and pour over the chocolate. Stir with a dry wooden spoon until the chocolate dissolves completely. If the hot cream fails to dissolve all the chocolate, put the mixture in bain-marie. Allow to cool for 15 minutes, then stir in the cherry purée. Store in the refrigerator.

Cherry coulis

Reserve four whole cherries for garnish. Slice the remaining cherries in two and remove pits. Purée half of the remaining cherries in the blender with a tablespoon of water, the sugar and lemon juice. Strain and cook over low heat for five minutes. Remove from heat and cool.
Use the rest of the cherries for presentation.

Presentation

Place two chocolate tablets on each plate. Cover with a layer of *ganache* and one of the seedless cherry halves. Repeat the assembly, finishing off with two chocolate tablets. Garnish with a whole cherry and drizzle with a ribbon of cherry coulis.

Agadir

Green figs with basil ice cream and pine-nuts

6 servings

Ingredients

Green figs
- 12 green figs, rinsed and dried
- 2 cups water
- 1 cup sugar

Basil ice cream
- 2 cups milk
- 20 fresh basil leaves
- 5 egg yolks
- ³/₄ cup sugar
- 1 cup heavy cream

Basil sauce
- 4 cups milk
- 15 fresh basil leaves
- 6 egg yolks
- 1 cup sugar

Garnish
- 6 basil leaves cut into thin strips
- ¹/₂ cup pine-nuts, roasted

Special equipment
- measuring cup
- ice cream machine

Preparation

Green figs

Rub the figs' skin with a small, fine sponge to remove the fuzz covering them, and make a cross cut on the top of each one. In a heavy-duty saucepan, heat the water and the sugar to boiling. Add the figs and cook over low heat for several hours, until figs are softened but still intact. If the syrup reduces more than desired, add hot water. Store figs in the syrup. For best flavor, the syrup must not be too thick.

Basil ice cream

Heat the milk with the fresh basil. When it comes to a boil, remove from heat, cool for 15 minutes, and pour off the milk, discarding the basil leaves. Beat the egg yolks with the sugar until pale and creamy. Add half the cream and mix well. Slowly whisk the hot milk into the beaten egg yolks and cream. Transfer to a heavy-duty saucepan and cook over low heat. Stir constantly with a wooden spoon, without letting boil, until the foam disappears from the surface and the mixture coats the back of the spoon. Remove from heat and strain into a bowl set over an ice bath. Stir in the rest of the cream. Cool and then chill completely. Pour into the ice cream machine and proceed according to the manufacturer's instructions. Store in the freezer until serving.

Basil sauce

Heat the milk and the basil until boiling. Remove from heat, cool for 15 minutes, and pour off the milk, discarding the basil. In a separate bowl, beat the egg yolks with the sugar until pale and creamy. Reheat the milk and whisk it slowly into the beaten eggs. Transfer the mixture to a heavy-duty saucepan and cook over low heat. Stir constantly with a wooden spoon, without letting boil, until the foam disappears from the surface and the mixture coats the back of the spoon. Strain in a bowl set over an ice bath and cool.

Presentation

Slice the figs in half and arrange four on each plate cut side up, imitating a four-leaf clover. Spoon out an ice cream *quenelle* and place on top. Drizzle with basil sauce. Sprinkle with the basil and the pine-nuts.

Brussels

Petits pots of celery, apple, and freesia

4 servings

Ingredients

Petits pots of celery

- 1 cup milk
- 2 celery stalks, rinsed and sliced crosswise
- 2 egg yolks
- ¼ cup sugar

Petits pots of apple

- 1 cup milk
- 1 green apple, rinsed, peeled, and sliced thinly
- 2 egg yolks
- ¼ cup sugar

Petits pots of freesia

- 1 cup milk
- ¼ cup freesia petals
- 2 egg yolks
- ¼ cup sugar

Garnish

- 2 celery stalks, rinsed and peeled
- 1 cup light syrup, see Appendix, page 181
- 1 green apple
- ¼ lemon
- 24 freesia petals

Special equipment

- measuring cup
- 12 individual ramekins, 5cm in diameter
- mandoline

Preparation

Petits pots of celery

Select 12 ramekins or custard pots, four for each flavored *petit pot*. In a saucepan, heat the milk with the celery until boiling. Remove from heat and cool for ten minutes. Purée in the blender and strain, discarding the celery.

In a bowl, beat the egg yolks with the sugar until pale and creamy. Reheat the milk, then slowly whisk it into the beaten egg yolks. Transfer the mixture to a heavy-duty saucepan and cook over low heat. Stir constantly with a wooden spoon, without letting boil, until the foam disappears from the surface and the mixture coats the back of the spoon. Strain in a bowl set over an ice bath and cool.

Preheat the oven to 250°F/121°C.

Pour the mixture in the ramekins, up to 1cm below the edge. Bake for 35 minutes. Turn off the oven and leave the ramekins inside for another ten minutes. Remove. Then cool thoroughly in the refrigerator.

Petits pots of apple

In a saucepan heat the milk with the apple until boiling. Remove from heat and cool for ten minutes. Purée in the blender and strain.

Proceed using the same method as for the petits pots of celery.

Petits pots of freesia

In a saucepan heat the milk with the freesia petals until boiling. Remove from heat and cool for ten minutes. Strain, discarding the petals.

Proceed using the same method as for the petits pots above.

Garnish

Celery

Cut the celery stalks in 5cm-long pieces. Slice into a julienne.

In a saucepan, combine the light syrup and the celery. Cook for ten minutes or until softened. Keep the sticks in the syrup and chill in refrigerator. Before serving, scatter the julienne of celery on the petits pots of celery.

Apple

With a mandoline slice the apple very thin. Rub with lemon to avoid browning and fan the slices out. Place on the petits pots of apple a little before serving.

Freesia

Boil the freesia petals in light syrup for a minute. Keep in the syrup until serving. Place on the petits pots of freesia.

Presentation

Decorate the petits pots with their corresponding garnishes. Serve three on each plate, one of each flavor.

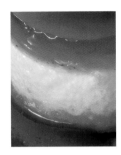

Kashmir

Basil textures with tamarind coulis

6 servings

Ingredients

Basil flan
- 2 cups milk
- 10 basil leaves
- 3 eggs
- 2 egg yolks
- 1 cup sugar

Basil jelly
- 1 leaf of gelatin
- 1 1/2 cups water
- pinch of salt
- 15 basil leaves
- 1 tablespoon basil leaves
- 1 tablespoon sugar
- 1 drop of green vegetable coloring

Tamarind coulis
- $1/4$ cup tamarind pulp
- $1/4$ cup water
- 1 tablespoon sugar

Vanilla génoise
- 3 eggs
- $1/3$ cup sugar
- 1 teaspoon vanilla extract
- $1/2$ cup sifted flour
- $1/2$ oz melted butter

Garnish
- 6 basil flowers

Special equipment
- kitchen scales
- measuring cup
- 6 metal rings, 6cm in diameter and 4cm high
- waxed paper
- pastry brush

Preparation

Basil flan

In a saucepan, combine the milk with the basil leaves; bring to a boil. Remove from heat and cool for ten minutes. Purèe in the blender and strain. In a separate bowl, beat the eggs, egg yolks and sugar until pale and creamy. Reheat the milk and whisk it slowly into the beaten eggs. Transfer the mixture to a heavy-duty saucepan and cook over low heat. Stir constantly with a wooden spoon, without letting boil, until the foam disappears from the surface and the mixture coats the back of the spoon. Strain into a bowl set over an ice bath and cool.

Basil jelly

Soak the gelatin in iced water until softened.
Boil the water with the salt, add the basil leaves and cook for two minutes. Remove from heat and allow to steep for five minutes. Add the sugar, purée in the blender and strain. Add the food coloring and the drained gelatin. Stir until gelatin is completely dissolved. Store at room temperature.

Tamarind coulis

Boil the tamarind pulp with water. Add the sugar and cook until thickened. Strain and cool. Store in refrigerator until serving.

Vanilla génoise

With the quantities indicated above, prepare the vanilla *génoise* following the recipe in the Appendix.

Assembly of flans

Preheat the oven to 250°F/121°C. Grease the six metal rings with vegetable oil. Place them on a sheet pan lined with waxed paper. Cut out six rounds of génoise the size of the rings, brush with the flan mixture, and insert in rings. Pour the flan mixture into the rings, up to 1cm below the rim. Bake for 35 minutes. Turn off the oven and leave flans inside for another ten minutes. Remove. After they have settled, chill thoroughly. Once chilled, top off the rings with the liquid jelly and garnish with a little basil flower. Chill until the jelly congeals completely.

Presentation

Take the flans out of the refrigerator, place in the center of each plate and slip out of the rings. Drizzle with a ribbon of tamarind sauce. Serve immediately.

Paris

Cinnamon tuiles filled with strawberry sorbet on red fruit

6 servings

Ingredients

Strawberry sorbet
- $5^1/_4$ oz strawberry purée
- $^1/_2$ cup water
- $^1/_4$ cup sugar
- 1 teaspoon lemon juice

Cinnamon tuiles
- 5 oz melted butter
- 1 cup sugar
- 1 cup flour
- $^7/_8$ cup coconut milk, see Appendix, page 179
- 1 tablespoon powdered cinnamon

Sugared roses
- 1 egg white
- 12 rose petals
- sugar for sprinkling

Raspberry coulis
- 1 cup raspberries
- 1 teaspoon sugar
- 1 tablespoon water
- 1 tablespoon lemon juice

Fruit
- 18 washed cherries
- 12 strawberries, halved lengthwise
- 12 blackberries, halved lengthwise
- 24 raspberries

Special equipment
- kitchen scales
- measuring cup
- ice cream machine
- *silpat* sheet
- waxed paper
- small paint brush

Preparation

Strawberry sorbet

Rinse the strawberries and remove stems. Halve, combine with the water, sugar, and lemon juice, and purée in the blender. Put the mixture in the ice cream machine and proceed according to the manufacturer's directions. Transfer the sorbet to a deep bowl and cover with plastic wrap. Store in the freezer until serving.

Cinnamon tuiles

Combine the melted butter and the sugar; mix well. Beat until creamy. Slowly add the flour and coconut milk. Continue beating until batter is smooth. Cover with plastic wrap and chill for one hour. Preheat the oven to 300°F/150°C. With a flexible spatula, spread the dough onto a silpat sheet, or onto a greased and floured sheet pan, forming a layer 2mm thick. Sprinkle the dough with the cinnamon. Bake for ten minutes or until golden. Remove from oven and cool for 30 seconds. With a sharp knife, cut the *tuiles* into 11x6cm rectangles. Wrap the tuiles around a cylindrical object 2cm in diameter. Overlap one end over the other and hold until the tuile cools completely. Carefully remove from the cylinder and store in an airtight container until using. Shape the tuiles in the same manner.
The tuiles must be warm for molding. If they have hardened a little when cooling, reheat in the oven for a few seconds, then mold quickly.

Sugared roses

Preheat the oven to 300°F/150°C. Line a sheet pan with waxed paper. Beat the egg white until foamy. With a small paint brush, dab the petals on both sides with the beaten egg white and sprinkle with sugar. Bake for 15 minutes until dry and lightly golden. Remove from oven and cool.

Raspberry coulis

Put the raspberries in the blender with the sugar, water, and lemon juice. Purée. Strain and store covered until serving.

Presentation

Form a base on each plate with the evenly distributed red fruit. Fill the cinnamon tuiles with strawberry sorbet. Garnish with rose petals and drizzle with a ribbon of raspberry coulis.

Hua Hin

Jasmine and lemongrass tea ice

8 servings

Ingredients

Tea ice

- 4 cups water
- 2 tablespoons jasmine tea leaves
- 6 tablespoons honey
- 4 stalks of lemongrass
- 20 fresh jasmine petals
- 8 mint leaves

Special equipment

- measuring cup
- 16x12cm rectangular baking pan

Preparation

Iced tea

Boil the water and pour immediately over the jasmine tea. Steep for five minutes, then strain, discarding the leaves. Add the honey, lemongrass stalks and jasmine petals, reserving eight petals for the tea ice. In a saucepan, simmer the mixture for ten minutes. Strain into a pitcher. Retrieve the petals from the sieve and put them back in the tea. Cool, then chill in the refrigerator.

Tea ice

Line the inside of the rectangular sheet pan with plastic wrap, pour in half a cup jasmine tea, and immerse the eight reserved petals. Freeze, making sure the pan remains exactly level in the freezer.

Presentation

Pour a little tea in eight clear glasses, distribute the jasmine petals among them and add a mint leaf to each. Remove the tea ice from the freezer. Cut in eight irregular pieces and use to garnish the tea glasses. Serve immediately.

Capri

Chocolate tortellini filled with mint cream

4 servings

Ingredients

Tortellini
- 1 egg
- 1 tablespoon water
- ¾ cup flour
- ¼ cup confectioners' sugar
- ⅜ cup unsweetened cocoa powder

Egg coating
- 1 egg
- pinch of salt

Mint cream filling
- see Appendix, page 181

Sugared petals
- 16 rose petals
- 1 egg white
- sugar for sprinkling

Port and roses caramel
- ½ cup sugar
- ½ cup port
- 4 drops of lemon juice
- 2 tablespoons rosewater

Garnish
- ¼ cup whole almonds
- *julienne of* rose petals

Special equipment
- measuring cup
- food processor
- biscuit cutter, 5cm in diameter
- pasta-making machine
- small paint brush

Preparation

Tortellini

Beat the egg with the water. Sift the flour with the sugar and cocoa. Combine everything in a food processor, pulsing just until dough comes together. Do not overprocess the dough, or it will toughen.

Shape the dough into a ball and wrap in plastic wrap. Chill for at least an hour. Take out of refrigerator and place on a slightly floured work surface. Roll the dough into a rectangle. Pass the dough through the pasta machine set at maximum thickness. Once this is done, fold the dough in three, and repeat the step three more times. Reduce the machine's setting gradually until set at minimum, passing the dough through the thinest setting several times. Spread the thinned dough over the work surface. With a biscuit-cutter 5cm in diameter, stamp out 16 circles. Cover lightly with plastic wrap.

Mint cream filling

Prepare the mint filling following the recipe in the Appendix.

Sugared petals

Preheat the oven to 300°F/150°C. Line a sheet pan with waxed paper. Beat the egg white until foamy. With a paint brush, dab the petals on both sides with the beaten egg white and sprinkle with sugar. Bake for 15 minutes until dry and lightly golden. Remove from oven and allow to cool.

Port and roses caramel

Mix the sugar, port and lemon. Cook over medium heat until reaching caramel thickness. Remove from heat and stir in the rose water.

Assembly

To make the egg coating, beat the egg and the salt together.

To shape the tortellini, pour a teaspoon mint cream filling onto each circle and brush half the edge with the beaten egg. Fold in half and close, pressing to seal. Once closed, gather together the extremities of the half-moon towards the middle, dab with the beaten egg and press together. Fill a pan with water and allow to boil. Put in the tortellini and cook for six minutes or until *al dente*. Remove with a skimming ladle, drain well and serve immediately.

Presentation

Garnish the plates with the almonds and sugared petals. Place four tortellini on top, drizzle a little caramel around, and scatter the juliènne of rose petals over the plate.

Montecarlo

Phyllo bundles with melted chocolate filling

4 servings

Ingredients

Chocolate filling
- 3¹/₂ oz dark chocolate, finely chopped
- ¹/₈ cup heavy cream
- 3 tablespoons *cognac*

Chocolate sauce
- see Appendix, page 178

Wrapping
- 2 sheets of *phyllo* dough
- clarified butter, see Appendix, page 179
- confectioners' sugar

Special equipment
- kitchen scales
- pastry brush

Preparation

Chocolate
Melt the chopped chocolate in bain-marie, taking care to keep the water from boiling. Remove from heat; stir in the cream and cognac. Mix thoroughly. Transfer the mixture to a clean, dry bowl, cover with plastic wrap and refrigerate until solid.

Chocolate sauce
Prepare the chocolate sauce following the recipe in the Appendix.

Dough
Preheat the oven to 350°F/175°C. When the chocolate mixture is firm, spread one of the phyllo sheets on a work surface, dab with clarified butter, and sprinkle with confectioners' sugar. Put another phyllo dough sheet on top and repeat. Cut the dough in four equal squares and put a tablespoon of chocolate filling in the center of each. To assemble the bundles, gather the corners of the square together, putting garble but firm pressure on the part with the filling. Use aluminium foil to support the shaped bundle. Spread the tips out in blossom-like fashion and bake the bundles for seven minutes or until lightly golden outside with the chocolate melted inside.

Presentation
Pour some chocolate sauce on the plate and place a bundle over it. Serve immediately.

Lucerne

Kahlua chocolates with raspberries and phyllo

4 servings

Ingredients

Kahlua chocolates

- 3 cups tempered bitter chocolate, see Appendix page 178
- $^1/_3$ cup heavy cream
- 3 tablespoons *Kahlua*
- $1^3/_4$ oz white chocolate

Chocolate filling

- 1 cup brown sugar
- 1 cup milk
- $1^3/_4$ oz butter
- $^3/_4$ cup flour
- 1 teaspoon ground cinnamon
- $^1/_2$ cup cocoa powder
- $^1/_4$ cup sugar

Phyllo

- 4 sheets of *phyllo* dough
- $^1/_2$ cup clarified butter, see Appendix, page 179
- $^1/_2$ cup confectioners' sugar

Blackberry and rose coulis

- $1^1/_2$ cups blackberries, stems removed and rinsed
- $^1/_2$ cup rosewater
- $^3/_4$ cup sugar

Garnish

- $^3/_4$ cup blackberries, washed
- 1 cup raspberries
- 16 red rose petals

Special equipment

- kitchen scales
- measuring cup
- small chocolate confectioner's molds
- offset spatula
- sheet of *silpat* or waxed paper
- baking pan
- baking sheet
- pastry brush
- candy thermometer
- 8 wooden skewers

Preparation

Kahlua chocolates

Temper the bitter chocolate, following the procedure in the Appendix. Then pour into the confectioner's mold, turn the mold over and, with three sharp taps, remove the excess. Chill until the chocolate hardens. In a saucepan, heat the cream, and stir in the Kahlua. Melt the white chocolate in bain-marie. Pour the cream and Kahlua mixture over the white chocolate and stir until thoroughly blended. Cool to 88°F/30°C. Make a waxed paper cone and fill with the white chocolate mixture. Fill the molds up to three quarters full. Chill for ten minutes. Then pour in more bitter chocolate, smooth the surface with an offset spatula and chill for 20 minutes. Unmold by gently rapping the mold over a surface.

Chocolate filling

Preheat the oven to 350°F/175°C. Grease and flour a baking pan. In a saucepan, mix the brown sugar, half the milk, and the butter. Cook over medium heat, stirring occasionally, until the butter melts and the sugar dissolves. Remove from heat. Sift the flour, cinnamon, and half the cocoa together; stir them in. When everything has dissolved, pour the mixture into the pan and smooth with spatula. Mix the remaining sugar and cocoa together; with a sieve, sprinkle over the top. Bake for 20 minutes.

Remove from the oven, pour in the remaining milk, and bake for an additional 15 minutes or until firm.

Phyllo bundle assembly

Preheat the oven to 350°F/175°C. Place one of the phyllo sheets on a sheet pan lined with waxed paper. Dab the phyllo with clarified butter. Sprinkle with confectioners' sugar. Set another sheet on top and repeat.

With a sharp knife, cut the phyllo dough sheets in four equal parts. Repeat the buttering and sprinkling procedure with the two remaining phyllo sheets. Pour a tablespoon of chocolate filling in the center of each of the eight squares, top with a Kahlua chocolate, and arrange a few blackberries and raspberries around it. Cover with another tablespoon of filling. Fold the dough into small square bundles, so the seam is hidden underneath. Arrange on a sheet pan, dab with clarified butter and sprinkle with confectioners' sugar. Bake for eight to ten minutes, taking care that the top layer doesn't burn.

Blackberry and rose coulis

Halve the blackberries. In a saucepan combine them with the water and the rosewater and bring to boil. Add the sugar and cook, stirring until dissolved. Purée in the blender and strain.

Presentation

Through each wooden skewer, thread two rose petals, one blackberry, and two raspberries. Use to garnish the warm bundles and drizzle with a ribbon of blackberry and rose coulis.

Almost indefinable, like the sensation of the hand touching and fondling silk, like images that fade away and only reveal outlines beyond the transparent veil that allows a glimpse of them, like a vague gesture, or words that name something without quite naming it, or a smell that one cannot at first identify, a subtle taste can carry us away for a brief moment before we recognize the nature of what we feel and perceive.

The desserts of this chapter were created in this spirit. There seems to exist poetics of taste in the subtle. The senses are challenged: what is expected to be bitterly sweet proves a mere insinuation of sweetness. Here everything is natural, without additives, to constitute the essence of sweet, acid, and sweet-and-sour together with herbs that tend neither towards warm nor cold.

Between the taste of nothing and a taste that one recognizes immediately, exists the possibility of a taste which is not exactly familiar yet not totally unfamiliar. A *sommelier* may sniff at a glass of wine and find the wine too young. This subtle exercise of the smell decides on the quality of the wine. The qualities of these desserts also appeal to the senses of smell, taste and sight and they should not be distracte. The tenderness put into the preparation of the desserts demands equal tenderness at the instant of savouring them. Subtlety and tenderness, in a nutshell. If tender is what has not yet ripened, subtle is that which is hard to define. When it becomes defined, taste must have been used in depth, just as sight is used in depth to discern the shapes of the landscape behind the curtains. A little mystery will always remain, as in the smile that made Mona Lisa's smile classical.

Sri Lanka

Earl Grey tea bavarois with watermelon strips

6 servings

Ingredients

Bavarois

- 3 leaves of gelatin
- 1 cup milk
- 2 tablespoons *Earl Grey* tea leaves
- 4 egg yolks
- 1/2 cup sugar
- 1 cup heavy cream
- vegetable oil for greasing

Watermelon strips

- 1/2 small watermelon

Earl Grey tea syrup

- 1/2 cup water
- 1/2 cup sugar
- 1 teaspoon Earl Grey tea leaves

Special equipment

- measuring cup
- 6 hexagonal molds 6.5cm wide and 5cm high
- mandoline

Preparation

Bavarois

Soak the gelatin in iced water until softened.

In a saucepan, heat the milk until boiling. Remove from heat and pour over the tea. Steep for ten minutes. Strain, discarding tea leaves.

In a bowl, beat the egg yolks with the sugar. Reheat the tea and milk infusion and pour over the beaten eggs and sugar, whisking constantly. Transfer the mixture to a heavy-duty saucepan and cook over medium heat. Stir constantly with a wooden spoon until the foam disappears from the surface and the mixture coats the back of the spoon. Do not allow to boil. Remove from heat. Transfer the mixture to a bowl set over an ice bath and chill. Drain the gelatin, add to the hot mixture and stir until completely dissolved. Cool.

Beat the cream until it forms soft peaks. Gently fold into the cooled tea mixture. To make a bottom for the metal molds, place each mold on a piece of plastic wrap, pressing the excess wrap to the outer surface.

Grease the molds with vegetable oil. Pour the *bavarois* in each one and chill for 30 minutes or until congealed.

Watermelon strips

Cut and peel the fruit, remove the seeds. With a mandoline, cut the pulp in very thin slices. Slice into rectangles and then into strips 1cm thick.

Earl Grey tea syrup

Boil the water with the sugar. Add the tea and simmer over low heat for a minute. Remove from heat and strain, discarding tea leaves. Store in the refrigerator.

Presentation

To unmold, peel the plastic wrap from the bottom of the molds. Wrap each mold in a hot kitchen towel, and gently ease the bavarois out into the center of each plate.

Garnish with watermelon strips and drizzle lightly with tea syrup.

Istanbul

Jasmine rice kebab with pineapple and watermelon

6 servings

Ingredients

Jasmine rice
- 1 tablespoon jasmine tea leaves
- 1 cup water, plus 2 tablespoons
- ¾ cup milk
- ¾ cup rice
- 2 tablespoons corn syrup

Fruit
- ¼ small watermelon
- ½ small pineapple
- 1 cup light syrup, see Appendix, page 181
- 2 tablespoons rum
- 2 tablespoons rock sugar

Garnish
- 12 jasmine flowers

Special equipment
- measuring cup
- mandoline

Preparation

Jasmine rice
Put the jasmine tea in a small bowl. Boil one cup of water and pour it over the jasmine tea. Steep for five minutes and strain, discarding the tea leaves.
In a saucepan, heat the jasmine tea and milk, until boiling. Add the rice and allow to cook over low heat until the rice is *al dente* and all the liquid is gone. Inmediately mix the corn syrup with the remaining water. Stir well and cook over low heat for another five minutes. Remove from heat; cool. Chill until serving.

Fruit
Carefully peel the watermelon so that only the rosy pulp remains. Remove the seeds. Peel the pineapple and make sure to remove the "eyes." With a mandoline, slice the fruit very thin. In a saucepan, heat the light syrup with the rum until boiling. Remove from heat; cool. Add the rock sugar and steep for 30 minutes or so.

Presentation
With the chilled rice, shape 12 rolls, 2cm thick and 7cm long. Place two rolls on each plate. Cover one with watermelon and the other with pineapple slices. Garnish with jasmine flowers and drizzle with a ribbon of rum syrup.

Rashid

Tangerine and star anise pyramid

4 servings

Ingredients

Anise syrup
- 2 cups water
- ½ cup sugar
- 6 whole star anise

Tangerines
- 6 small tangerines, peeled, white pith and fibers removed

Tangerine cream
- 2 leaves of gelatin
- 1 1/2 cups tangerine juice
- 4 whole star anise
- ½ cup sugar
- 4 eggs
- 2⅛ oz butter

Garnish
- 1 tangerine, peeled, white pith and fibers removed, segments separate

Special equipment
- kitchen scales
- measuring cup
- 4 individual pyramid-shaped molds

Preparation

Star anise syrup
In a saucepan, boil the water with the sugar and star anise. Remove from heat and cool. Extract the star anise pieces and reserve them for garnish.

Tangerines
Separate the tangerines in segments. Boil the segments over very low heat in the anise syrup for 20 minutes. Remove from heat and allow to steep.

Tangerine cream
Soak the gelatin in iced water until softened.
In a saucepan, heat the tangerine juice with the star anise and sugar until boiling; boil three or four minutes. Strain and put in bain-marie. Add the eggs one by one, whisking constantly, until the mixture is smooth and thick. Remove from heat, add the butter and stir well. Drain the gelatin, dissolve in a little of the warm mixture and add to the rest of the preparation. With the cream, fill the four pyramid-shaped molds halfway. Add a layer of tangerine segments, and finish off with the tangerine cream. Refrigerate until completely firm.

Presentation
Take the pyramid molds out of the refrigerator, place one in the middle of each plate and let them slip out. Garnish with the tangerine segments on one side and the reserved star anise on the other.

Tahiti

Papaya cannelloni with orange mousse and caramel sauce

6 servings

Ingredients

Orange mousse
- 1 leaf of gelatin
- 1 cup Italian meringue, see Appendix, page 180
- 2 cups orange juice
- ½ teaspoon corn starch

Caramel sauce
- ½ cup water
- 1 1/2 teaspoons corn syrup
- ¼ cup sugar
- 3 tablespoons heavy cream
- 2 tablespoons butter

Papaya cannelloni
- 6 Hawaiian papayas

Syrup
- ¼ cup light syrup, see Appendix, page 181

Special equipment
- measuring cup
- mandoline

Preparation

Orange mousse
Soak the gelatin in iced water until softened.
Prepare the Italian meringue following the recipe in the Appendix.
In a saucepan, cook the orange juice over medium heat until reduced by half. Add the corn starch and stir the mixture constantly until it thickens. Remove from heat, add the drained gelatin and stir until thoroughly dissolved. Strain and fold gently into the Italian meringue. Chill the mousse for at least half an hour. Keep refrigerated until serving.

Caramel sauce
Prepare an ice water bath. In a heavy-duty saucepan, combine the water, corn syrup, and sugar. Cook over high heat until the caramel turns dark golden. Remove from heat and plunge the bottom of the pan in cold water to shock, taking care not to let any water droplets into the pan. Stir in the cream and resume cooking. Stir constantly, cooking over heat until all the bits of hardened caramel have dissolved again. Remove from heat and stir in the butter. Store at room temperature. Before serving, heat in bain-marie.

Papaya cannelloni
Carefully peel the papayas and remove the seeds. Just before serving, cut very thin slices lengthwise with a mandoline. You will need at least 30 similarly-sized slices.

Syrup
Prepare syrup according to recipe in Appendix.

Presentation
In the center of each papaya slice, put a teaspoon of orange mousse and a trickle of caramel sauce, and roll to form cannelloni. Place five on each plate. Dab the papayas with some of the light syrup to give them a sheen. Drizzle with caramel sauce.

Yucatán

Sapodilla sorbet

6 servings

Ingredients

Sapodilla sorbet

- 15 *sapodillas*
- ½ cup water
- ¼ cup sugar

Garnish

- 1 cup sugar
- ½ cup water
- 3 tablespoons corn syrup
- 12 whole almonds, shelled
- 3 tablespoons sapodilla purée

Special equipment

- measuring cup
- ice cream machine
- *silpat* sheet or waxed paper
- candy thermometer

Preparation

Sapodilla sorbet

Peel the sapodillas. Remove the pit and scrape out pulp with a knife. Purée in the blender. Strain to get rid of fibers and reserve three tablespoons of purée for presentation. Weigh the purée to make sure you have the 5 1/8 oz needed for the sorbet. Stir in the water and sugar. Process in the ice cream machine, following the manufacturer's intructions. Transfer the sorbet to a deep bowl and cover with plastic wrap. Store in the freezer until serving.

Garnish

Fill a deep bowl with ice water. In a heavy-duty saucepan, mix the sugar, water, and corn syrup. Cook over high heat until the mixture reaches 250°F/121°C or the hard ball stage. Plunge the bottom of the pan into the ice bath to shock. To make the almond buds, hold a tip of the almond between your fingers and dip it halfway into the caramel. Remove gently, letting the caramel harden to form the stem. Lay on a sheet of silpat or waxed paper to cool. Repeat with all the almonds.

Presentation

With a teaspoon, scoop out *quenelle*-shaped scoops of sorbet. Place two on each plate. Garnish with two almond buds and a few drops of sapodilla purée.

Delhi

Jasmine and lilac savarin

8 servings

Ingredients

Jasmine sorbet

- 2 cups water
- 1 tablespoon jasmine tea leaves
- 50 fresh jasmine flowers
- $^3/_8$ cup sugar
- $^1/_8$ cup corn syrup
- 1 teaspoon lemon juice
- 2 tablespoons of fresh lilac blossoms

Vanilla génoise

- 3 eggs
- $^1/_3$ cup sugar
- 1 teaspoon vanilla extract
- $^1/_2$ cup sifted flour
- 1 tablespoon butter

Sauces

- $^1/_2$ cup crème anglaise, see Appendix, page 180
- 2 tablespoons blackberry coulis, see Appendix, page 176

Special equipment

- measuring cup
- ice cream machine
- 8 individual *savarin* molds

Preparation

Jasmine sorbet

Put the jasmine tea in a small bowl. Boil the water and pour over the tea. Steep for five minutes and strain, discarding the tea leaves. Add the jasmine flowers, sugar, corn syrup, lemon juice, and lilac petals, and reheat until the mixture begins to boil. Remove from heat and cool. Retrieve a few jasmine and lilac flowers, and reserve them for garnish. Put the mixture in an ice cream machine, and process according to the manufacturer's directions. Transfer the sorbet to a deep bowl and cover with plastic wrap. Store in the freezer.

Vanilla génoise

With the quantities indicated above, prepare the vanilla *génoise* following the recipe in the Appendix, page 184.

Sauces

Prepare the custard and the blackberry coulis following the recipes in the Appendix.

Assembly

Put some of the reserved flowers at the bottom of each little savarin mold and fill with jasmine sorbet. Cut a round of génoise the diameter of the savarin mold and use it to cover the sorbet. Store the molds in the freezer.

Presentation

To unmold, quickly dip each savarin in warm water. Invert each onto the plate and slip the savarin out of the mold. Drizzle with the custard, the blackberry coulis, and scatter a few flowers around. Serve immediately.

Saint Tropez

Honey bavarois in tuile nests with kiwi and prickly pears

6 servings

Ingredients

Honey bavarois

- 3 leaves of gelatin
- 2 cups milk
- 6 tablespoons honey
- 4 egg yolks
- 2 tablespoons sugar
- $^1/_2$ cup heavy cream

Tuile nest

- vegetable oil for greasing
- $1^3/_4$ oz butter
- $^3/_8$ cup confectioners' sugar
- 2 egg whites
- $^5/_8$ cup flour

Fruit

- 2 kiwis
- 2 prickly pears

Special equipment

- kitchen scales
- measuring cup
- 2 metal cylinders, 6cm in diameter
- *silpat* sheet
- 40x30cm rectangular mold
- pastry comb
- melon baller
- nozzleless pastry bag

Preparation

Honey bavarois

Soak the gelatin in iced water until softened.

In a saucepan heat the milk until boiling, and add the honey. Mix well and remove from heat.

Beat the egg yolks with the sugar and whisk in the milk and honey mixture. Cook over moderate heat, stirring with a wooden spoon until the foam disappears from the surface and the mixture coats the back of the spoon. Do not allow to boil. Remove from heat.

Strain the preparation into a bowl set over an ice bath. Drain the gelatin, add it to the honey and milk mixture, and stir until completely dissolved. Cool. Beat the cream until it forms soft peaks, and gently fold into the honey *bavarois* mixture.

Place the bavarois in the refrigerator for an hour or until congealed.

Biscuit nest

Preheat the oven to 300°F/150°C. Grease the metal cylinders with vegetable oil.

Cream the butter, add the sugar and beat with an electric mixer creamy. Gradually add the egg whites, beating constantly. At this point, the mixture tends to separate: this is normal. Finally, add all the flour at once and continue beating until the batter is smooth. Chill the batter for at least half an hour. With a metal spatula, spread a third of the batter over a silpat sheet or onto a greased and floured rectangular sheet pan, forming two 20x10cm rectangular layers, each with an even thickness of 1mm. Shape fine threads by passing the pastry comb along the length of each, leaving a 2.5cm uncombed margin at one end. Bake for eight to ten minutes until golden, and remove from oven. To shape the tuile nest, wrap the warm threads around a greased cylinder and hold until cooled. Carefully detach from cylinder. Repeat the operation with the other biscuit threads. With the rest of the dough, prepare another four nests in the same manner.

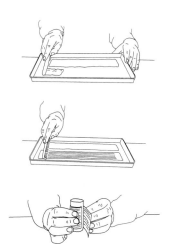

Fruit

Peel the kiwis and prickly pears. With a melon baller, cut out fruit balls 1cm in diameter.

Presentation

Place a tuile nest in the center of each plate. With a nozzleless pastry bag or a spoon, fill the nests with honey bavarois. Garnish with the fruit balls.

Damascus

Baked plums with apricot compote

6 servings

Ingredients

Chocolate génoise
- ½ cup sugar
- 4 eggs
- ½ cup sifted flour
- ¼ cup cocoa in powder form
- 1 oz melted butter, cooled slightly

Filling
- 10 apricots in syrup
- 6 red plums
- 6 sprigs of fresh oregano

Special equipment
- kitchen scales
- measuring cup
- medium-sized sheet pan
- waxed paper
- blender

Preparation

Chocolate génoise

Preheat the oven to 350°F/175°C. In a heavy-duty saucepan, combine the eggs and sugar and put in bain-marie. Do not let temperature of water exceed 120°F/50°C. Whisk constantly with an electric or manual beater until the mixture doubles in volume. Remove the pan from the water bath. Sift the flour and cocoa together. Fold gradually into the beaten eggs. Finally, mix the melted butter with a tablespoon of batter and combine with the rest of the mixture. Pour onto the sheet pan lined with waxed paper. Smooth the surface with a flexible spatula until forming a layer no thicker than 2mm, and bake for eight minutes. Remove from oven, cool for 30 seconds, and peel the waxed paper from the bottom of the *génoise*. With a sharp knife, cut out six 11x3 rectangles. Wrap the warm biscuit around a cylindrical object, leaving 2.5cm free at one end. Hold until cools and hardens. Carefully detach from the cylinder and store in an airtight container until using. Mold all rectangles in the same fashion. The tuiles must be warm for molding. If they have hardened a little when cooling, reheat in the oven for a few seconds, then mold quickly.

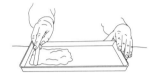

Filling

Preheat the oven to 200°F/94°C. Drain the apricots and reserve the syrup. Remove and discard the pits; purée the flesh in the blender. Strain, cover and keep in refrigerator. Make a small triangular incision in the bottom of plums to remove the pit. Place the plums on a baking sheet lined with waxed paper and bake for about 15 minutes or until the skin begins to wrinkle. Remove from oven and peel. Cool the cherries and dab them with the reserved apricot syrup.

Presentation

Place a génoise cylinder on each plate. Fill with the apricot compote. Put a syrup-coated plum on top and garnish with a sprig of oregano set next to the plum.

Vienna

Feijoa napoleon with Dubonnet cream

4 servings

Ingredients

Dough
- 3 sheets of *phyllo* dough
- ¼ cup clarified butter, see Appendix, page 179
- ¼ cup confectioners' sugar

Dubonnet cream
- 1 cup *Dubonnet*
- 1 1/2 cups milk
- 4 egg yolks
- ¼ cup sugar
- ⅓ cup sifted flour
- 1³⁄₈ oz butter

Feijoas
- 4 *feijoas*

Special equipment
- kitchen scales
- measuring cup
- sheet pan
- *silpat* sheet or waxed paper
- mandoline

Preparation

Dough
Preheat the oven to 350°F/175°C.
Place one of the phyllo dough sheets on a sheet pan lined with a silpat sheet or waxed paper, dab with clarified butter, and sprinkle with confectioners' sugar sifted through a sieve.
Repeat the process, layering on the two remaining phyllo dough sheets.
With a knife, cut six equal squares and then divide diagonally to get 12 triangles. Bake the triangles for five minutes or until golden. Remove from oven and cool.

Dubonnet cream
Heat the Dubonnet and boil until reduced by half.
Heat the milk until boiling; remove from heat. In a bowl, beat the egg yolks with the sugar until pale and creamy. Add the flour, beating constantly. Slowly pour the hot milk over the mixture, whisking constantly. Transfer to a heavy-duty saucepan and cook over low heat until thickened, beating constantly.
Remove from heat; add the reduced Dubonnet and the butter. Mix well. Pour the Dubonnet cream into a bowl, cover with plastic wrap, and cool. Store in the refrigerator.

Feijoas
Shortly before serving, rinse the feijoas and, with a mandoline, slice very thin.

Presentation
Place a phyllo triangle in the middle of each plate. Cover with a teaspoon of Dubonnet cream and a few feijoa slices. Assemble three on each plate.

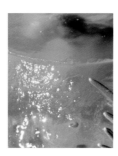

Côte d'Or

Prune jelly with Grand Marnier

6 servings

Ingredients

Prune jelly

- 4 leaves of gelatin
- vegetable oil for greasing ring molds
- ½ cup seedless prunes
- 2 cups water
- 2 cups orange juice
- ¼ cup *Armagnac*
- ¼ cup *Grand Marnier*

Optional garnish

- 6 sprigs of rosemary or other aromatic herb

Special equipment

- measuring cup
- 6 metal rings, 6cm in diameter and 3.5cm high, or 12 smaller ones.

Preparation

Prune jelly

Soak the gelatin in iced water until softened.

Grease the inner surface of the metal rings with vegetable oil. To give them a bottom, place each ring on a piece of plastic wrap and press the excess wrap onto the outer surface. Place in the refrigerator.

Cook the prunes in the water until the liquid reduces to half. Remove from heat and cool. Mix the orange juice with the Armagnac and boil for a minute. Drain the prunes and add their liquid to the orange juice and Armagnac. Add the drained gelatin and stir until completely dissolved. Purée the prunes in the blender.

Remove the molds from the refrigerator, pour in a small quantity of the jelly mixture, tilting the molds to cover the inner surface and the bottom with an even layer. Chill for a few minutes until the jelly congeals thoroughly. Remove from refrigerator and spoon a little prune purée into the bottom of each mold. Cover with a little more jelly and refrigerate again until congealing. Continue alternating layers of purée and jelly until the molds are filled, refrigerating to firm each layer. Finish off with a layer of jelly and store molds in the refrigerator until before serving.

Presentation

To unmold the jelly, detach the plastic wrap and wrap the ring in a warm kitchen towel. Place in the center of the plate, lift slightly and let the jelly slip out. Spoon a teaspoon of Grand Marnier on top. If you like, garnish with a sprig of rosemary or another aromatic herb of your choice.

Bahía

Baskets of crisp mango and Amaretto aspic with orange coulis

4 servings

Ingredients

Amaretto aspic
- 3 leaves of gelatin
- 1 cup *Amaretto*
- ¹/₂ cup orange juice

Crisp mango
- 2 mangoes
- 1 cup light syrup, warmed, see Appendix, page 181

Orange coulis
- 1 cup orange juice
- 1 tablespoon sugar
- 1 tablespoon corn starch

Special equipment
- measuring cup
- rectangular mold or baking pan
- mandoline
- baking sheet
- waxed paper

Preparation

Amaretto aspic
Soak the gelatin in iced water until softened.
Combine the Amaretto and orange juice in a saucepan, and cook over medium heat, stirring until reduced by half. Remove from heat. Drain the gelatin and stir it thoroughly into the mixture. Strain and pour into a rectangular mold or baking pan. Refrigerate for half an hour or until firm. Just before serving, cut with a knife into tiny cubes.

Crisp mango
Preheat the oven to 250°F/121°C. Rinse the mangoes and, with a mandoline, cut 16 very thin slices. Steep the mango slices in the hot syrup for five minutes, making sure they remain well soaked. Carefully place the mango slices on a sheet pan lined with waxed paper and bake until lightly golden. Remove from oven and shape little baskets by wrapping each slice around a wine cork or similarly shaped object wrapped in aluminium foil. Hold until hardened. Store the mango baskets in an airtight container so they remain crisp.

Orange coulis
In a saucepan, combine the orange juice with the sugar and cook over medium heat until reduced by half. Add the corn starch, stirring until slightly thickened. Remove from heat, strain and cool.

Presentation
Place four little mango baskets on each plate and fill with the Amaretto aspic cubes. Serve with a little orange coulis spooned on the side.

Ascot

Rice pudding with apple and lemon tea

6 servings

Ingredients

Rice pudding

- 1 1/2 cups milk
- 1 cup water
- 1 tablespoon apple and lemon tea
- 1/2 cup rice
- 1 egg
- 2 tablespoons sugar
- 1/2 cup heavy cream

Lemon tea sauce

- 2 cups milk
- 2 tablespoons lemon tea leaves
- 3 egg yolks
- 1/2 cup sugar
- 1/2 teaspoon vanilla extract

Blackberry coulis

- see Appendix, page 176

Garnish

- 1 red apple
- 1 lemon

Special equipment

- measuring cup
- 6 hexagonal ring molds, 6.5cm wide and 5cm high
- mandoline

Preparation

Rice pudding

Preheat the oven to 300°F/150°C. In a saucepan, combine a cup of the milk, the water and the tea leaves; heat until boiling. Remove from heat, steep for five minutes and strain, discarding tea leaves. Reheat the milk. Add the rice, stir, and cook over low heat until dry. In a bowl, beat the egg with the sugar; add the rest of the milk and the cream. Pour over the cooked rice and stir gently. Grease the hexagonal ring molds with melted butter, fill them with the rice pudding, and place in a baking dish. Boil a little water and pour into the dish, so the water comes half a centimeter up the sides of the of the hexagonal molds. Bake the molds in their water bath for 20 minutes. Remove and cool. Store in the refrigerator until serving.

Lemon tea sauce

In a saucepan, combine the milk with the lemon tea; boil for two minutes. Remove from heat, steep for five minutes, and strain, discarding the leaves. In a bowl, beat the egg yolks with the sugar and vanilla extract until pale and creamy. Slowly whisk the hot milk into the beaten eggs. Transfer the mixture to a heavy-duty saucepan and cook over low heat. Stir constantly with a wooden spoon, without letting boil, until the foam disappears from the surface and the mixture coats the back of the spoon. Strain into a bowl set over an ice bath and cool.

Blackberry coulis

Prepare the blackberry coulis following the recipe in the Appendix.

Presentation

Take the molds out of the refrigerator and gently let the contents slip into the center of each plate. With a mandoline, cut the apple in very thin slices, squeezing a little lemon juice over them to avoid browning. Garnish the pudding with the apple slices. Drizzle a ribbon of the blackberry coulis and the lemon tea sauce around, and serve.

Borneo

Mango tower with poppy seeds

4 servings

Ingredients

Mango filling
- 1 1/2 leaves of gelatin
- 4 mangoes, peeled and cut in chunks
- 3 tablespoons sugar
- 1 tablespoon poppy seeds

Phyllo
- 3 sheets of *phyllo* dough
- clarified butter,
  see Appendix, page 179
- confectioners' sugar

Sugared flowers
- 4 fresh violets
- 1 egg white
- 1 tablespoon sugar

Vanilla and poppy seed caramel
- 2 tablespoons water
- $^1/_4$ cup sugar
- 1 tablespoon corn syrup
- 1 teaspoon vanilla extract
- 1 teaspoon poppy seeds

Special equipment
- blender
- 2 square baking pans, 30x30cm
- sheet pans
- *silpat* sheet
- pastry brush
- waxed paper

Preparation

Mango filling

Soak the gelatin in iced water until softened.
Purée the mangooes in a blender. Strain the purée and add the poppy seeds. Stir in the drained gelatin and mix well. Pour into baking pans and chill for half an hour or until congealed.

Phyllo

Preheat the oven to 300F°/150C°.
Put one of the phyllo dough sheets on a sheet pan covered with silpat or waxed paper. Brush it with clarified butter and sprinkle with confectioners' sugar. Repeat the process with the two remaining sheets, placing one on top of the other.
With a sharp knife, cut twelve 6cm squares. Bake for five minutes or until golden. Cut the remaining phyllo into strips half a centimeter wide and place on wrinkled aluminium foil to give a wavy, irregular shape. Bake for five minutes or until golden. Remove from heat; cool.

Sugared flowers

Preheat the oven to 300°F/150°C.
Line a sheet pan with waxed paper. With a fork, beat the egg white until foamy.

With a small paint brush, brush the flowers on both sides with the beaten egg white and sprinkle with sugar. Bake on the sheet pan for 15 minutes until dry and lightly golden. Remove from oven; cool.

Vanilla and poppy seed caramel

Prepare a cold water bath. In a heavy-duty saucepan, mix the water, sugar, corn syrup, and vanilla extract. Cook over medium heat until very pale yellow. Remove from heat and plunge the bottom of the pan in the cold water bath to halt the cooking. Add the poppy seeds and stir well with a wooden spoon.
Before serving, heat in a bain-marie.

Presentation

Take the mango filling out of the refrigerator and cut into 12 5cm squares. In the middle of each plate, alternately stack caramelized phyllo and mango squares, until forming a three-layer stack. Garnish with the wavy phyllo strips, a sugared flower, and a little caramel sauce on the side.

Borinquen

Crunchy pears with banana mousse

4 servings

Ingredients

Banana mousse
- 2 leaves of gelatin
- 3^1/$_2$ oz Italian meringue, see Appendix, page 180
- 5^1/$_4$ oz bananas
- 1 tablespoon lemon juice
- ^{3}/$_4$ cup heavy cream

Crunchy pear
- 4 large pears, rinsed
- 2 cups light syrup, see Appendix, page 181

Caramelized banana
- 1 fresh banana
- 2 tablespoons butter
- 1 teaspoon corn syrup
- 2 tablespoons sugar

Chocolate sauce
- ^{1}/$_2$ cup chocolate sauce, see Appendix, page 178

Special equipment
- kitchen scales
- measuring cup
- 4 metal rings, 6cm in diameter
- mandoline
- *silpat* sheet
- sheet pans
- waxed paper

Preparation

Banana mousse

Soak the gelatin in iced water until softened.

Prepare the Italian meringue following the recipe in the Appendix.

Arrange the metal rings on a sheet pan lined with waxed paper.

Peel the bananas, removing all fibers, and purée thoroughly in the blender. Add the lemon juice. Drain the gelatin, heat slightly in a saucepan until completely dissolved, add to the banana, and mix. Fold in the Italian meringue. Beat the cream until it forms soft peaks, and gradually fold it into the banana mixture. Pour the mousse into the metal rings; chill until congealed. Store in the refrigerator until serving.

Crunchy pear

Preheat the oven to 200°F/94°C.

With a mandoline, cut 36 very thin slices lengthwise. Cook over low heat in the light syrup until transparent. Remove from heat. Fish out the slices, shaking off excess syrup, and arrange on a silpat sheet or on a sheet pan lined with waxed paper. Bake until dry and golden. Remove from oven. To shape, roll each slice around a pencil or similarly thin cylindrical object. Cool then, carefully detach and store in an airtight container to retain crispness.

Caramelized banana

Slice the banana crosswise half a centimeter thick. In a frying pan over medium heat, combine the butter, corn syrup, and sugar. When the mixture comes to a boil, add the banana slices. Sauté, shaking the pan occasionally to caramelize the slices evenly, until the bananas are browned.

Chocolate sauce

Prepare the chocolate sauce following the recipe in the Appendix.

Presentation

Place a ring on each plate and let the mousse slip out. Cover with caramelized banana slices and surround with crunchy pears. Finish with a thin ribbon of chocolate sauce.

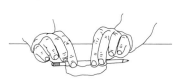

As convention goes, the classical is the part of human creation that has withstood the test of time. The classical is the object of admiration, imitation or study. The classical, all in all, resists fashion, which, on the contrary, changes with the rhythm of tastes or whims of those who make it. The classical has a recognizable seal of identity: in general, restraint and balance; in art, style where one can recognize epochs and cultures, and lengthy periods of creativity.

It is not easy to pay tribute to the classical in the great domain of cuisine. But it is possible to do so insofar as recipes, flavors and styles have remained in the memory of taste, as the memory of taste is one of the characteristics of the gourmet. One acknowledges as familiar a taste one has savoured for a long period of time. Common speech refers to it as the "classical taste of…" In other words: the classical is recognizable —neither unusual nor surprising. What about *pâtisserie?* Is there such a thing as classical *pâtisserie?* Certainly, and among the great schools of cuisine in the world, the "classicism" of French *pâtisserie* bears a unique and permanent mark that these desserts wished to recall and emulate.

This is not a transcript of the classical, but rather, classicism is a source of inspiration. In this section, one recognizes the savours and styles that French *pâtisserie* has made its own for centuries. I have not intended to proffer anything new, but to execute something new, thanks to the lessons provided by a style and a manner of dessert making.

If the classical is "imitable", it is not faithful imitation that motivates these creations. It is reminiscence, tribute, and inspiration based on well-known formulas, and a certain touch of restraint that does not shun the need to create new desserts with classical inflections within the *répertoire* of this book.

Cahuinari

Cold crème brûlée with corn

4 servings

Ingredients

Crème brûlée

- 2 leaves of gelatin
- 2 1/2 cups canned sweet corn
- ½ cup heavy cream
- 1 tablespoon sugar
- ½ cup brown sugar

Special equipment

- measuring cup
- 4 ramekins or custard molds, 8cm in diameter and 5cm high
- mini blowtorch

Preparation

Crème brûlée

Soak the gelatin in iced water until softened.
Purée the sweet corn in the blender.
Add the cream and sugar. Process again in the blender until the mixture is smooth. Drain the gelatin and mix it with a little of the strained corn purée. Stir it thoroughly into the rest of the corn purée.
Pour the custard into the ramekins and refrigerate for an hour.

Presentation

Just before serving, take molds out of the refrigerator. Invert ramekins onto a serving plate and unmold. Sprinkle with brown sugar and caramelize the surface with a mini blowtorch. Serve immediately.

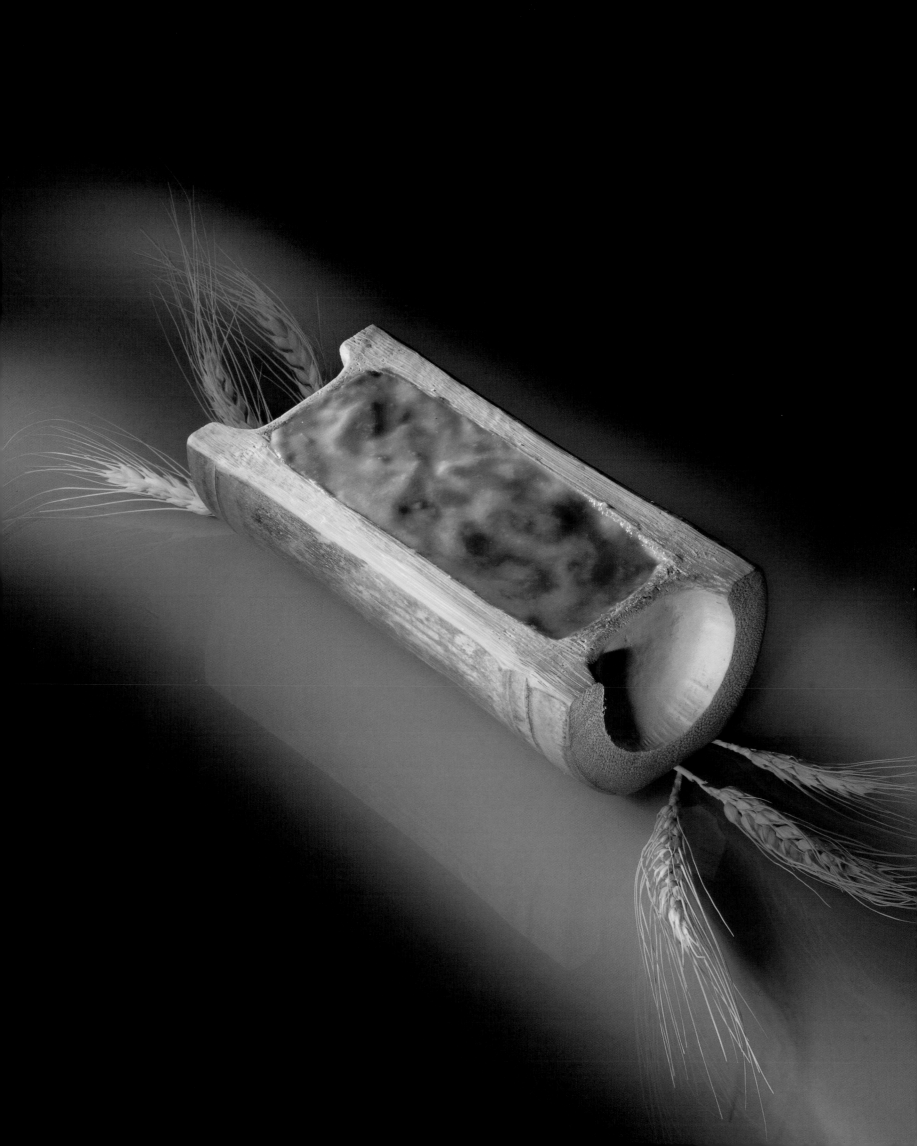

Mazatlán

Thyme and chocolate soufflés

6 servings

Ingredients

Thyme cream
- 2 cups milk
- 2 sprigs of fresh thyme
- 4 egg yolks
- $^3/_8$ cup sugar
- $^1/_3$ cup sifted flour
- $1^3/_8$ oz butter

Soufflé
- $^1/_2$ cup grated dark chocolate
- 6 egg whites
- $^1/_2$ cup sugar
- butter and sugar for the molds

Special equipment
- kitchen scales
- measuring cup
- 6 individual *soufflé* molds, 6cm
  in diameter

Preparation

Thyme cream

In a saucepan, combine the milk and the thyme. Heat until boiling; simmer for five minutes. Remove from heat and steep for ten minutes. Purée in the blender and strain. In a bowl, beat the egg yolks with the sugar until pale and creamy. Add the flour, beating constantly. Slowly whisk the hot milk into the mixture, whisking constantly. Transfer to a heavy-duty saucepan and cook over low heat until thickened, stirring constantly to avoid lumps. Remove from heat and add the butter. Mix well. Transfer to a bowl, cover with plastic wrap and cool. Store at room temperature.

Soufflé

Preheat the oven to 375°F/190C° Grease and sugar the molds. Fold the chocolate into the thyme cream. In a separate bowl, beat the egg whites and sugar until foamy. Fold the beaten egg gently into the cream. Pour the mixture into the individual soufflé molds. Bake for eight to ten minutes, until the soufflés rise and are lightly browned.

Presentation

Remove the soufflés from oven and serve immediately.

Lancashire

Babas with red fruit tea

8 servings

Ingredients

Babas

- ⅔ oz fresh yeast
- 2 tablespoons warm water (approximately)
- pinch of salt
- 2 1/2 cups sifted flour
- ⅛ cup sugar
- 3 eggs
- 2⅛ oz butter cut into cubes, at room temperature
- melted butter

Red fruit tea

- 4 tablespoons red fruit tea leaves
- 3 cups water
- 4 tablespoons sugar
- ¾ cup rum

Garnish

- a flower of your choice

Special equipment

- kitchen scales
- measuring cup
- 8 *baba* molds, 5cm in diameter

Preparation

Babas

In a bowl, mix the yeast with the hot water. Add the salt.
Add the flour, sugar, and eggs; beat with an electric mixer, until the dough feels elastic. Add the butter and mix well.
Brush the inside of the baba molds with melted butter.

Distribute the dough among the baba molds. Let the babas proof in a warm draft-free place for around 20 minutes, until they fill with the swelling dough. Preheat the oven to 375°F/190°C and bake for 20 to 30 minutes, or until cooked and golden.
Unmold the babas immediately onto a wire cake rack and cool.

Red fruit tea

Put the red fruit tea leaves in a bowl. In a saucepan, combine the water, sugar, and rum, and heat until boiling. Pour immediately over the red fruit tea. Steep for five minutes. Return the tea to the saucepan, boil again, and plunge the babas into the tea. Cook the babas for eight minutes. Remove and drain on a rack placed over a deep dish. Reserve the tea for garnish and store the babas in the refrigerator.

Presentation

Place a baba in the middle of each dish and splash with a little tea. Garnish with a flower of your choice.

Boston

White chocolate and blueberry tartelette

4 servings

Ingredients

Tart shells
- 3^1/$_2$ oz butter
- ^{7}/$_8$ cup confectioners' sugar
- pinch of salt
- 1 egg yolk
- 1 egg
- 2 tablespoons hot milk
- 2 1/2 cups sifted flour

White chocolate mousse
- 1 1/2 leaves of gelatin
- ^{1}/$_2$ lb of white chocolate
- 1 1/2 cups heavy cream
- 2 cups blueberries, rinsed

White chocolate sauce
- 3^1/$_2$ oz white chocolate
- ^{1}/$_4$ cup milk

Special equipment
- kitchen scales
- measuring cup
- 4 circular tart pans, 10cm in diameter and 2cm high
- pastry bag
- candy thermometer

Preparation

Tart shells

Soften the butter in your hands. Transfer to a bowl and combine thoroughly with the confectioners' sugar, salt, egg yolk, egg and milk. Gradually add the flour and knead until dough is smooth, taking care not to overwork the dough. Shape into a ball, wrap in plastic wrap and cool in the refrigerator for at least an hour. Grease and flour the tart pans. Sprinkle a work surface with flour. Take the dough out of the refrigerator and divide into four equal parts. With a rolling pin, roll out each into a round, with an even thickness of 2mm. Ease the dough into the tart pans, pushing gently with your fingertips. Put the tart pans in the refrigerator for 15 minutes.
Preheat the oven to 350°F/175°C. Remove the tart pans from the refrigerator and prick each a few times with a fork. Bake for 10 to 12 minutes or until golden. Unmold over a rack and cool at room temperature.

White chocolate mousse

Soak the gelatin in iced water until softened.
Melt the white chocolate in a bain-marie. Remove from heat, add half the cream, and stir well. Keep the rest of the cream in the refrigerator. Drain the gelatin, dissolve it in a little of the hot melted chocolate, and add to the rest of the preparation.

With an electric mixer, beat the rest of the cream until it forms semi-firm peaks. Fold the cream into the white chocolate mixture when the white chocolate cools to a temperature of 115°F/45°C. Reserve the blueberries for assembly.

White chocolate sauce

Melt the white chocolate in a bain-marie. Add the milk and mix well. Strain the sauce into a glass bowl for easy heating before serving. Cover with plastic wrap and keep at room temperature.

Assembly

With a pastry bag, fill the tart shells with the white chocolate mousse. Cover the entire surface with the blueberries. Store in the refrigerator until serving.

Presentation

Heat the white chocolate sauce. Pour a little on each plate and set a tartelette on top.

Naples

Strawberry and grape millefeuille in balsamic vinegar

8 servings

Ingredients

Fruit
- 48 strawberries
- 32 green grapes
- $^1/_4$ cup sugar
- $^1/_4$ cup balsamic vinegar

Lemon cream
- $1^1/_3$ cups condensed milk
- $1^1/_3$ cups heavy cream
- 1 cup lemon juice
- 1 tablespoon grated lemon rind

Millefeuille
- $^1/_2$ lb of millefeuille dough
  see puff pastry, Appendix, page 182
- 1 teaspoon corn syrup
- 2 tablespoons water
- confectioners' sugar for sprinkling

Balsamic vinegar caramel
- $^1/_4$ cup sugar
- $^1/_4$ cup balsamic vinegar
- 1 tablespoon butter

Special equipment
- kitchen scales
- measuring cup
- *silpat* sheet
- 40x30cm rectangular mold
- metal skewer

Preparation

Fruit
Wash the strawberries and halve them lengthwise.
Peel the grapes, cut in half, and remove seeds.
Dissolve the sugar in the balsamic vinegar and macerate the fruit in the vinegar mixture for two hours.

Lemon cream
In a blender combine the condensed milk, cream, and lemon juice; process briefly to mix thoroughly. Pour into a bowl and stir in the grated lemon rind. Refrigerate for two hours.

Millefeuille
Prepare the millefeuille dough following the recipe in the Appendix.
Preheat the oven to 450°F/230°C.
With a rolling pin, spread the millefeuille over a lightly floured work surface and form a 40x30cm rectangle 2mm thick. Prick the dough with a fork to prevent swelling. Mix the corn syrup with the water and brush over the surface of the millefeuille. Bake for five minutes. Remove from oven, flip the millefeuille over and brush the other side with the syrup. Bake for another five minutes. Repeat on both sides to caramelize the millefeuille evenly. Remove from the oven. Trim the edges until you have a 36x24cm rectangle. Divide into twenty four 6cm squares.

To make the tops, decorate eight squares by covering each millefeuille square with a layer of confectioners' sugar. With a red-hot metal skewer, trace four diagonal lines across the sugared top, making a burnt-sugar design. Heat the skewer again, turn the tops 45 degrees, and trace another four diagonal lines to form a lattice pattern.

Balsamic vinegar caramel
Mix the sugar, balsamic vinegar and a tablespoon of water. Cook over medium heat until the mixture acquires the desired caramel thickness. Remove from heat, and add the butter.

Presentation
Place one millefeuille square in the middle of each plate. Cover with one teaspoon of the lemon cream. Place the six strawberries at the edges of the square. Fill the center with four grapes so they are even with the strawberries. Cover with another millefeuille square. Repeat the operation and finish off with the patterned tops. Pour a ribbon of caramel around.

Lausanne

Vanilla tuiles, chocolate mousse, strawberries, and starfruit

4 servings

Ingredients

Tuiles
- $2^5/_8$ oz butter
- $^5/_8$ cup confectioners' sugar
- 3 egg whites
- $^1/_2$ cup flour
- powdered cocoa

Chocolate mousse
- $7^7/_8$ oz semi-sweet chocolate
- $^1/_3$ cup heavy cream
- 2 egg yolks
- $^1/_8$ cup sugar
- 5 egg whites

Chocolate sauce
- $^1/_2$ cup chocolate sauce, see Appendix, page 178

Garnish
- 1 cup strawberries cut in half lengthwise
- 1 cup *starfruit* sliced into 3mm thick stars
- 4 mint sprigs

Special equipment
- kitchen scales
- measuring cup
- *silpat* sheet
- 30x40cm sheet pan
- candy thermometer

Preparation

Tuiles

Melt the butter and add the sugar. Beat until creamy. Gradually add the egg whites, beating constantly. At this point, the mixture tends to separate: this is normal. Finally, throw in all the flour at once and continue beating until batter is smooth. Cover with plastic wrap and refrigerate for one hour.

Preheat the oven to 300°F/150°C. With a metal spatula, spread the dough over a silpat sheet or in a greased and floured sheet pan to an even thickness of 1mm. Trace a cross in the center to divide the dough into four equal squares. Sprinkle the dough with the cocoa powder and bake for six to eight minutes, until golden. Remove and cool for 15 seconds. To shape the tuiles, detach each by raising a corner. Join this corner with the opposite corner. Hold the two corners for a few seconds until they keep their shape after cooling. The biscuit must be warm to be molded. If it has hardened a little when cooling, heat again in the oven for a few seconds, then mold rapidly.

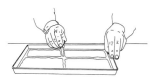

Chocolate mousse

Melt the chocolate in a bain-marie, stirring occasionally to ensure even melting. When the chocolate is melted, add the cream, mix well and remove from the heat. In a separate bowl, beat the egg yolks with 2/3oz of the sugar until pale and creamy. Add the chocolate and mix well. Beat the egg whites with the rest of the sugar until foamy. Heat the chocolate to 105°F/40°C and fold into the rest of the preparation.

Chocolate sauce

Prepare the chocolate sauce following the recipe in the Appendix.

Presentation

Place a *tuile* on each plate. Accompany with chocolate mousse and garnish with the strawberries, starfruit, chocolate sauce, and mint sprigs.

Bogotá

Floating islands

8 servings

Ingredients

Sesame sauce
- 2 cups milk
- 4 tablespoons roasted sesame seeds
- 3 egg yolks
- ¹/₂ cup sugar

Chocolate sauce
- ¹/₂ lb of unsweetened chocolate, finely chopped
- ¹/₂ cup heavy cream
- 3 tablespoons corn syrup
- 1 teaspoon vanilla extract

Floating islands
- ¹/₂ cup water
- 1 1/2 cups sugar
- 4 egg whites
- 2 tablespoons roasted sesame seeds

Poaching liquid
- 4 cups milk
- 4 tablespoons sugar

Special equipment
- kitchen scales
- measuring cup

Preparation

Sesame sauce

In a saucepan, combine the milk and three tablespoons of the roasted sesame. Remove from heat and cool for ten minutes. Purée in the blender and strain. In a bowl, beat the egg yolks with the sugar until pale and creamy. Slowly whisk the hot milk into the beaten egg yolks, beating constantly. Transfer the mixture to a heavy-duty saucepan and cook over low heat. Stir constantly with a wooden spoon, without letting boil, until the foam disappears from the surface and the mixture coats the back of the spoon. Strain into a bowl set over an ice bath and cool. Stir in the remaining sesame seeds.

Chocolate sauce

Put the chocolate in a deep bowl. In a saucepan, heat the cream with the corn syrup and vanilla extract until boiling. Pour over the chocolate and mix until the chocolate melts completely and is smooth. If the hot cream fails to dissolve all the chocolate, put the mixture in a bain-marie.

Floating islands

In a heavy-duty saucepan, heat the water with the sugar until the sugar dissolves completely and the mixture becomes a syrup. Remove from heat, clean the rim of the pan with a wet pastry brush, and cook to eliminate all the foam on the surface. Continue cooking over high heat until the mixture reaches 250°F/121°C or the hard ball stage.

With an electric mixer, beat the egg whites until foamy. Reduce speed to low and add the syrup in a thin trickle. When all the syrup has been blended in, turn the speed to high until the mixture cools completely. This should take about five minutes. Add the roasted sesame seeds. Reserve the meringue at room temperature.

Poaching

Combine the milk and the sugar in a heavy-duty saucepan and bring to a boil. Reduce the heat to simmer. With two soup spoons, shape 12 *quenelles* with the reserved meringue. Slip the quenelles into the hot milk and poach for three minutes, turning them over halfway through cooking. Remove carefully with a skimming ladle, gently pat dry with a clean kitchen towel and serve immediately as explained below.

Presentation

Pour a little chocolate sauce and sesame sauce on each plate, place two meringue quenelles over the sauces, and sprinkle with toasted sesame. Serve immediately.

Avignon

Fruit gratin in zabaglione

4 servings

Ingredients

Fruit

- 1 banana
- 2 kiwis
- 8 strawberries
- 8 *uchuvas*
- 2 *feijoas*
- 2 tablespoons *agrás*

Zabaglione

- 1 egg
- 1 egg yolk
- ½ cup sugar

Special equipment

- measuring cup
- 4 individual ovenproof plates

Preparation

Fruit

Peel and cut the banana in thin crosswise slices. Cut each slice in two. Peel and cut the kiwis in thin slices. Cut each slice in two. Wash the strawberries and remove stems. Cut in halves lengthwise, and then in quarters. Wash the uchuvas and cut in halves. Wash the feijoas, remove the ends, cut in thin slices, and then cut each slice in two. Wash the agrás.

Zabaglione

Place the broiler pan in the upper position. Preheat the broiler. Mix the egg with the egg yolk and sugar. Pour in a saucepan, put the saucepan in a bain-marie, and beat until the mixture doubles in volume. Keep the bain-marie at 120°F/50°C.

Optionally, the zabaglione can be flavored with two tablespoons of poire, kirsch, or framboise stirred in before you cook them in the bain-marie.

Presentation

Distribute the fruit in four small gratin dishes. Cover with two tablespoons of zabaglione and brown under the broiler flame until golden. Serve immediately.

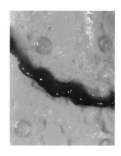

Oslo

Kiwi parfait glacé with strawberry mousse

4 servings

Ingredients

Kiwi parfait glacé
- see Appendix, page 180

Strawberry mousse
- see Appendix, page 183

Vanilla génoise
- 3 eggs
- $1/3$ cup sugar
- 1 teaspoon vanilla extract
- $1/2$ cup sifted flour
- $1/2$ oz melted butter

Assembly
- 12 chocolate tablets 4x4cm, see Appendix, page 178

Garnish
- $1/4$ cup raspberry jam
- $1/4$ cup peach jam
- confectioners' sugar
- 4 tablespoons *agrás*

Special equipment
- kitchen scales
- measuring cup
- plastic pastrysheets
- 30x40cm sheet pan
- *silpat* sheet

Preparation

Kiwi parfait glacé
Prepare the kiwi *parfait* glacé following the recipe in the Appendix.

Strawberry mousse
Prepare the strawberry mousse following the recipe in the Appendix.

Vanilla génoise
With the quantities indicated, prepare the vanilla *génoise* following the recipe in the Appendix, page 184. Once this is done, cut out four circles the diameter of the bottom of the cones to be filled with the parfait and the mousse.

Chocolate tablets
Prepare the chocolate tablets according to the recipe in the Appendix.

Assembly
To form the base of the little trees, with a sharp heated knife, cut out four chocolate segments in circles the diameter of the cones, and eight segments diagonally to obtain 16 right-angled triangles. Quickly heat one of the right-angled sides of the triangles and stick four by four to form the foot. With a little melted chocolate, stick the circles to the foot. To shape the molds for the cones, cut plastic as shown in picture. In each mold, spread an even layer of parfait 1cm thick. Put in the refrigerator for 15 minutes or until the mixture firms thoroughly. Remove from refrigerator and close the cones with adhesive tape. Smear a little more parfait on the seam

to fasten well. Allow to harden again in the refrigerator. Then fill the inside of the cones with strawberry *mousse* and, lastly, a round of génoise. Cover with plastic wrap and refrigerate for at least an hour.

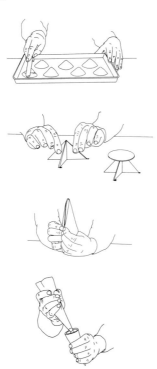

Presentation

Place a little chocolate tree on each plate. Take the parfaits out of the refrigerator, place over the chocolate circle on top and detach the plastic. With a cone of waxed paper filled with raspberry jam, trace a spiral around each parfait. Fill another cone with peach jam and scatter even dollops over the entire surface. Sprinkle confectioners' sugar around and garnish with agrás.

San Francisco

Chocolate macaroons and chocolate ganache with mint

6 servings

Ingredients

Chocolate macaroons
- 4³/₈ cups confectioners' sugar
- ⁵/₈ cup cocoa powder
- 3⁷/₈ cups ground almonds
- 7 egg whites

Chocolate and mint cream
- 1 cup heavy cream
- 4 sprigs of fresh mint
- ¹/₂ lb of bitter chocolate, finely chopped

Mint caramel
- 1 cup *crème de menthe*

Special equipment
- kitchen scales
- measuring cup
- medium-sized sheet pan
- pastry bag

Preparation

Chocolate macaroons

Preheat the oven to 500°F/260°C. Line the sheet pan with waxed paper. In a bowl, mix 15 3/4 oz of the confectioners' sugar, the cocoa powder and the ground almonds. Beat the egg whites until foamy, and add the rest of the sugar gradually to keep a matte color. Mix the rest of dry ingredients together and fold into the egg whites. Fit a pastry bag (with flat nozzle 1 cm in diameter) and fill it with the batter. Placing the nozzle obliquely on the waxed paper, squeeze evenly to avoid formation of air bubbles and pipe a round of the desired size for each macaroon. Repeat until filling the sheet pan, leaving a 2cm space in between each macaroon. Put in the oven and immediately reduce temperature to 350°F/175°C. Bake for about 15 minutes. Remove from oven, lift a corner of the waxed paper and pour one quarter of a cup of cold water underneath the paper. This will make the macaroons easier to detach and soft inside. Place the panful of macaroons on a rack and cool. The measures indicated yield more macaroons than necessary for six people but these are the minimum quantities recommended for success of the recipe: it is difficult to prepare macaroons in smaller quantities. The batter must be used immediately. However, once baked, macaroons can be frozen or kept in an airtight container for one week.

Chocolate and mint cream

In a saucepan, simmer the cream and mint for five minutes, without letting boil. Remove from heat and steep for ten minutes. Strain and reheat. Pour over the chocolate. Stir well until all the chocolate has melted and has completely blended with the cream. If the hot cream fails to dilute all the chocolate, put the mixture in a bain-marie. Refrigerate until the chocolate hardens.

Mint caramel

In a saucepan, boil the crème de menthe over medium heat, reducing until you get a thick, almost toffee-like consistency. Remove from heat.

Presentation

In the middle of each plate, set a macaroon domed side down. With the edge of a heated metal spoon, slowly scrape and scoop the chocolate and mint cream, exerting even pressure, until shaping a *quenelle*. Put two quenelles on each of the six macaroons. Sprinkle the other six macaroons with cocoa powder and, one by one, stick a cocoa-coated macaroon to those with the quenelles on top, forming a 45° angle. Garnish with a sprig of fresh mint and drizzle with a ribbon of mint caramel.

Samarkand

Pistachio and red fruit blinis

4 servings

Ingredients

Pistachio sauce
- 2 cups milk
- 1 tablespoon pistachio paste
- 3 egg yolks
- 1/2 cup sugar
- 2 tablespoons crushed pistachios

Blinis
- 1 egg yolk
- 1/4 cup sugar
- 2 tablespoons pistachio paste
- 1 cup sifted flour
- 1 teaspoon baking powder
- 1 cup milk
- 1 tablespoon melted butter
- 1 egg white
- 1 tablespoon sugar

Red fruit
- 8 cherries, rinsed
- 8 strawberries, rinsed and halved lengthwise, stems removed
- 16 raspberries
- 12 blackberries, rinsed and halved lengthwise, stems removed
- 2 tablespoons *agrás,* rinsed

Special equipment
- measuring cup
- non-stick frying-pan

Preparation

Pistachio sauce
In a saucepan heat the milk, mix the pistachio paste with a little of the milk and return it to the saucepan. Heat until boiling; remove from heat. In a bowl, beat the egg yolks with the sugar until pale and creamy. Reheat the milk, and whisk it slowly into the beaten egg yolks. Transfer the mixture to a heavy-duty saucepan and cook over low heat. Stir constantly with a wooden spoon, without letting boil, until the foam disappears from the surface and the mixture coats the back of the spoon. Strain into a bowl set over an ice bath and cool. Before serving, stir in the crushed pistachios.

Blinis
With a whisk, blend the egg yolk, sugar and pistachio paste in a deep bowl. Add the flour and baking powder. Beating constantly to avoid lumps, gradually add the milk. The mixture must become liquid and thick. Stir in the butter and cool in the refrigerator for half an hour. Beat the egg white with the sugar until foamy and gently fold the batter.
Heat a non-stick frying pan. Spoon the batter into the pan in 5cm rounds. Brown well on both sides. Serve immediately, as indicated below.

Presentation
Place four *blinis* on each plate and garnish with the fruit, and pistachio sauce. If desired, sprinkle the blinis lightly with confectioners' sugar.

Chartres

Chocolate terrine with ginger and lemon cream

10 servings

Ingredients

Ginger and lemon cream

- ³/₄ cup lemon juice
- 1 ginger root, peeled and sliced
- 1 tablespoon grated lemon rind
- ³/₄ cup sugar
- 4 eggs
- 4³/₈ oz butter

Chocolate cake

- 1 cup water
- ⁵/₈ cup cocoa powder
- 1 1/2 cups sifted flour
- 1 teaspoon baking powder
- pinch of baking soda
- 1 teaspoon salt
- 4³/₈ oz butter
- 1 cup sugar
- 3 eggs

Ginger sauce

- 2 cups milk
- 2 fresh ginger roots, peeled and sliced
- 3 egg yolks
- ¹/₂ cup sugar

Little lemon halves

- see Appendix, page 181

Special equipment

- kitchen scales
- measuring cup
- 2 *terrine* molds, 20x7cm
- pastry bag

Preparation

Ginger and lemon cream

In a pan, heat the lemon juice with the ginger; boil for five minutes. Strain and add the grated lemon rind and the sugar. Boil again, reduce the heat to a simmer and whisk in the eggs, stirring constantly, until the mixture thickens. Remove from heat, and, still beating constantly, gradually add the butter. Cover with plastic wrap and cool.

Chocolate cake

Preheat the oven to 350°F/175°C. Lightly grease and flour the terrine molds, reserving one for assembly later on. Boil the water and slowly whisk in the cocoa. Mix well and remove from heat. Sift the flour with the baking powder, baking soda, and salt.
Put the butter in a deep bowl and beat until creamy. Add the sugar and mix thoroughly. Then add the cocoa and water mixture in three passes, alternating with the sifted dry ingredients. Add the eggs one by one and beat until completely combined. Pour the mixture into the mold and bake for 45 minutes or until a cake tester comes out clean when inserted in the center. Cool for 15 minutes, unmold and cool completely.

Ginger sauce

In a saucepan heat the milk with the ginger, boil for two minutes. Remove from heat, cool for 15 minutes, and strain. In a bowl, beat the egg yolks with the sugar until pale and creamy. Boil the milk again and slowly whisk into the beaten egg yolks. Transfer the mixture to a heavy-duty saucepan and cook over low heat. Stir constantly with a wooden spoon, without letting boil, until the foam disappears from the surface and the mixture coats the back of the spoon. Strain into a bowl set over an ice bath and cool.

Little lemon halves

Prepare the little lemon halves following the recipe in the Appendix.

Terrine assembly

Line the terrine molds with plastic wrap. Cut a layer of chocolate cake 1cm thick and place it at the bottom. Spread a layer of ginger and lemon cream and cover with another 1cm layer of chocolate cake. Repeat the operation and finish off with another 1cm layer of cake. Chill for an hour.

Presentation

Slice off each end of the terrine and cut the rest in ten 2cm thick slices. Place one slice in the middle of each plate. Garnish with ginger sauce on one side and little lemon halves on the other.

London

Cherry and chocolate bread pudding

8 servings

Ingredients

Bread pudding
- 2 eggs
- ¹/₄ cup sugar
- ¹/₄ cup sifted flour
- 1 cup *crème anglaise*, see Appendix, page 180
- ¹/₂ cup blackberry coulis, see Appendix, page 176
- 2¹/₃ oz brownie, see Appendix, page 177
- 2¹/₃ oz *brioche,* see Appendix, page 176
- 1 cup grated semi-sweet chocolate
- 1 cup seedless cherries

Chocolate sorbet
- 3¹/₄ cup water
- ¹/₂ cup milk
- ³/₄ cup sugar
- ¹/₈ cup corn syrup
- ¹/₃ cup unsweetened cocoa powder
- 3¹/₂ oz grated semi-sweet chocolate

Cherry sauce
- 1 cup cherries, rinsed
- 1 tablespoon water
- 1 teaspoon sugar
- 1 teaspoon lemon juice

Special equipment
- kitchen scales
- measuring cup
- 8 ring molds, 6cm in diameter and 4cm high
- ice cream machine

Preparation

Bread pudding

Preheat the oven to 350°F/175°C.
In a bowl, beat the eggs with the sugar. Add the flour and mix well. Gradually fold in the crème anglaise and the blackberry coulis, stirring constantly. Crumble in the brownie and the brioche. Cover the bowl and allow to rest for one and a half hours. Stir in the grated chocolate and seedless cherries, making sure ingredients are evenly distributed. Grease the rings and place on a sheet pan lined with waxed paper. Fill the ring molds to the brim with the bread pudding and bake for 30 minutes or until firm. Remove from oven and cool.

Chocolate sorbet

In a saucepan, boil the water, milk, sugar, and corn syrup. Add the cocoa, beating constantly. When everything is blended, remove from heat and add the grated chocolate. Continue beating until the chocolate melts completely. Strain and cool. Process the mixture in an ice cream machine according to the manufacturer's instructions. Transfer the sorbet to a deep bowl and cover with plastic wrap. Store in the freezer until serving.

Cherry sauce

Slice the cherries in two and remove the pits. Purée half of them in the blender with the water, the sugar and the lemon juice. Strain and cook over low heat for five minutes. Remove from heat, add the rest of the cherries, and cool.

Presentation

Unmold the bread puddings and serve them hot with a scoop of chocolate sorbet on top and a ribbon of cherry sauce drizzled alongside.

Neuchâtel

Melted chocolate and rose cake

6 servings

Ingredients

Rose ice cream
- see Appendix, page183

Chocolate cake
- 2¹/₂ oz butter at room temperature
- 3 egg yolks
- ¹/₂ cups bitter chocolate, melted
- ³/₈ cup ground almonds
- ¹/₄ cup sifted flour
- ¹/₂ cup corn starch
- 3 egg whites
- ¹/₃ cup sugar

Chocolate and rose filling
- ¹/₂ cup heavy cream
- 12 rose petals
- 1 tablespoon rose water
- 2⁷/₈ oz milk chocolate, finely chopped

Chocolate sauce
- see Appendix, page 178

Special equipment
- kitchen scales
- measuring cup
- 6 ring molds, 12cm in diameter and 5cm high
- pastry bag
- ice cream machine
- waxed paper

Preparation

Rose ice cream

Prepare the rose ice cream following the recipe in the Appendix.

Chocolate cake

Preheat the oven to 325°F/165°C. Grease the six ring molds. Line the inside with a strip of greased and floured waxed paper sticking out one centimeter beyond the edge.

With an electric beater, beat the butter and egg yolks until creamy. Add the melted chocolate and mix well. Throw in the ground almonds, flour, and corn starch, and stir until batter is smooth. In a separate bowl, beat the egg whites until foamy and add the sugar gradually to keep its matte color. Gently fold into the chocolate mixture.

Place the metal rings in a sheet pan lined with waxed paper. Fill the rings to the middle and bake for eight minutes. Keep the remaining dough at room temperature. Remove the cakes from oven and press the dough down with the tips of your fingers, to form the base of the pastry. Cool the cakes in their molds.

Chocolate and rose filling

Heat the cream with the rose petals, without letting boil. Remove from heat and steep for ten minutes. Strain and add the rose water. Reheat the cream and pour over the milk chocolate. Stir until the chocolate is completely diluted. If the hot cream fails to melt all the chocolate, put the mixture in a bain-marie. Refrigerate the mixture until firm.

Assembly of cakes

Put a teaspoon of chocolate cream at the center of each cake base and cover with the remaining unbaked dough, filling the molds to the brim. Freeze for at least two hours.

Chocolate sauce

Prepare the chocolate sauce following the recipe in the Appendix.

Presentation

Preheat the oven to 350°F/175°C. Remove the cakes from the freezer. Bake for 12 minutes. Allow to cool for a minute before serving.

Place a chocolate cake in the center of each plate, peel off the waxed paper. Garnish with chocolate sauce, a scoop of rose ice cream and a few rose petals.

Appendix

Additional recipes

These preparations are part of some of the recipes featured in this book. When the quantities required are different from those in this appendix, the measures appear in the original recipe.

Crocantes de manzana

Agrás coulis

Yields ¹/₂ cup

Ingredients
- 3¹/₂ oz *agrás*
- 2 tablespoons sugar
- 1 tablespoon water

Special equipment
- measuring cup

Preparation
In a blender, purée the agrás with the sugar and the water. Strain, then cook over low heat for five minutes. Remove from heat and cool.

Angel hair

Ingredients
- 1 cup sugar
- ¹/₂ cup water
- 3 tablespoons corn syrup
- vegetable oil for greasing the forks

Special equipment
- measuring cup

Preparation
In a deep bowl prepare an ice bath. On a work surface position two tall tumblers 30cm apart to serve as lateral supports for the threading.
In a heavy-duty saucepan, mix the sugar, water and corn syrup. Cook over high heat until the mixture reaches 250°F/121°C, or the hard ball stage. Plunge the bottom of the pan into the bath to shock.

Working quickly, grease two forks with a little vegetable oil and hold them in one hand so they look like a

single eight-pronged fork. Dip them in the syrup, remove and with strong wrist movements, swing swiftly from left to right between the supports, to form the caramel threads for molding the nests. The threads will be suspended between the two lateral supports. Repeat until obtaining the desired quantity of angel hair. If the syrup cools, it can be heated again in a bain-marie. The syrup is delicate and crystallizes easily during cooking or during sugar thread making. To avoid, refrain from stirring or using syrup that has crystallized Angel hair can be prepared a few days ahead and stored, unmolded, in an airtight container.

Arequipe

Yields 3 cups

Ingredients
- 6 cups fresh milk
- 7$\frac{1}{2}$ cups sugar
- 1 shallot
- pinch of baking soda

Special equipment
- measuring cup

Preparation
Boil the milk, then add the sugar and shallot. The shallot, strange as it may seem, confers a very special flavor to the sweet. Mix well with a wooden spoon. At the moment it begins to thicken, add the baking soda and remove the shallot. Beat constantly with lengthwise movements of the spoon, always scraping the bottom of the pan. When the bottom of the pan starts showing at every scrape of the spoon, remove from heat and pour into an ovenproof container. Do not scrape the residue that sticks to the pan; it will crystallize.

The *arequipe* must have a dark golden gloss.

This is the minimum quantity of arequipe suggested to prepare. Leftover arequipe will keep in the refrigerator for up to a week.

In Colombia, arequipe is often used to accompany stewed blackberries and fig preserve.

Blackberry coulis

Yields $\frac{1}{2}$ cup

Ingredients
- $\frac{1}{2}$ lb of blackberries, rinsed and dried, stems removed
- 1 tablespoon sugar, or to taste

Special equipment
- kitchen scales

Preparation
In a blender, purée the blackberries with the sugar until smooth and thick. Strain and cook over low heat for five minutes. Remove from the heat and cool.

Brioche

Yields 600g

Ingredients
- 1 tablespoon lukewarm water
- 2 teaspoons fresh yeast
- 1 tablespoon sugar
- 1 teaspoon salt
- 2 cups sifted all-purpose flour
- 4 eggs
- 6$\frac{1}{3}$ oz butter, cut in cubes, at room temperature

Special equipment
- kitchen scales
- measuring cup
- 20x20cm baking pan

Preparation
In a deep bowl, combine the water and fresh yeast; mix until the yeast is completely dissolved. Add the sugar, salt, sifted flour and eggs. Beat until the dough is supple and smooth. Add the butter slowly and beat until the dough is smooth and elastic. Shape the dough into a ball, place in a bowl and cover with a cloth. Allow to rise at room temperature for half an hour or until doubled in bulk. Then punch the dough down with your hand, shape into a ball again, seal it in plastic wrap and refrigerate for at least two hours before shaping.

Preheat the oven to 400°F/ 205°C. Shape the dough as desired, and let it proof in the baking pan until almost doubled in bulk. Brush with egg and make a cross incision on top. Bake small brioches for eight to ten minutes and large brioches for 20 to 25 minutes, until deep golden. Brioche dough can be kept refrigerated for 24 hours or frozen for up to a

Brownie

Yields 16 brownies

Ingredients
- 5¼ oz dark chocolate, chopped
- 5⅛ oz butter
- 1 and ¾ cups sugar
- 3 eggs
- 1 1/2 teaspoons vanilla extract
- ⅔ cup sour cream
- 1 cup flour

Special equipment
- kitchen scales
- measuring cup
- 30x30cm baking pans
- waxed paper

Preparation
Preheat the oven to 350°F/175°C.
Grease the baking pans and line the bottom with waxed paper. Melt the chocolate and butter in a bain-marie. Remove from heat, add the sugar and, beating constantly, add the eggs one by one. Add the vanilla extract and sour cream; add the flour and mix just until thoroughly blended. Bake for 25 to 30 minutes, and avoid overcooking. Cool and cut in the fashion desired.

Chocolate génoise

Yields two 30x40cm layers

Ingredients
- 7 eggs
- 1 cup sugar
- 1 cup sifted sugar
- ⅝ cup unsweetened cocoa powder
- ⅛ cup melted butter, slightly cooled

Special equipment
- kitchen scales
- measuring cup
- 2 sheet pans 30x40cm
- *silpat* sheet

Preparation
Preheat the oven to 350°F/ 175°C.
In a deep bowl, beat the eggs with the sugar and vanilla extract until pale and creamy. Put in a bain-marie and beat constantly until the mixture doubles in volume. Do not let water temperature exceed 120°F/50°C. Remove the bowl from the warm water. Sift the flour and cocoa together and gradually fold into the beaten eggs. Thoroughly mix the melted butter with a tablespoon of the batter; fold into the rest of the preparation. Take care not to beat excessively or the batter will lose volume. Pour into the greased and

floured pans, lined with a *silpat* sheet. Spread the batter evenly with a metal spatula. Bake for ten minutes or until light golden. Remove from oven, and cool at room temperature.

Chocolate glaze

Yields 100g

Ingredients
- 3½ oz dark chocolate, finely chopped
- ⅓ cup vegetable oil

Special equipment
- kitchen scales
- measuring cup

Preparation
Gently heat the vegetable oil and pour over the chocolate. Stir until the chocolate is completely melted. If the hot oil fails to melt all the chocolate, put in a bain-marie. In order to glaze, the chocolate must be 88°F/30°C. Transfer the glaze to a clean container, cover with plastic wrap and store at room temperature.

Chocolate sauce

Yields 3 cups

Ingredients
- ½ lb of dark chocolate, finely chopped
- ½ cup heavy cream
- 3 tablespoons corn syrup
- 1 teaspoon vanilla extract

Special equipment
- kitchen scales
- measuring cup

Preparation
Put the chopped chocolate in a deep bowl. In a separate saucepan, combine the cream, corn syrup, and vanilla extract and bring to a boil. Pour the mixture over the chocolate and stir until the chocolate melts completely and the mixture is smooth. If the hot cream fails to dissolve all the chocolate, put the mixture in

Chocolate tablets

Yields 24 4x4cm tablets

Ingredients
- ⅔ lb of chocolate temper, see next recipe

Special equipment
- kitchen scales
- *rodoid* strips 4cm wide

Preparation
Over the plastic *rodoid* strips, spread the chocolate temper evenly in a 2mm thick layer . Use an offset spatula. Refrigerate until the chocolate hardens. To make the tablets, cut into 4cm strips with a sharp, dry, heated knife. Wait to detach the chocolate tablets from the plastic until serving.

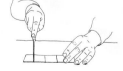

Chocolate temper

Through this process, chocolate is heated and cooled to induce a chain reaction where cocoa butter crystals form: this is known as sowing crystal seeds. The tempering stabilizes the chocolate and gives it a smooth gloss, long shelf life, and snap. Generally, chefs prefer to temper a chocolate coating that contains an average of 34 per cent cocoa butter and 40 per cent chocolate liqueur or pure chocolate.

There are two basic methods for tempering chocolate: sowing crystal seeds or table tempering. In the first method, chocolate cut in small pieces is put in a bain-marie in a dry, stainless steel bowl, the pan bottom should not touch the water. The chocolate is stirred until it melts and reaches the correct maximum temperature: 110°F/43°C for dark or semi-sweet chocolate, 105°F/41°C for milk chocolate, and 100°F/ 38°C for white chocolate. After it is removed from heat, the bottom of the bowl is dried to prevent the

Clarified butter

chocolate from absorbing humidity. A block of cold chocolate is then added (one pound for every five pounds of melted chocolate), and the mixture is periodically stirred until temperature is reduced to 88° to 90°F/32°C for dark or semi-sweet chocolate, 85° to 87°F/29°C for milk chocolate, and 83° to 84°F/28°C for white chocolate. When the mixture reaches the indicated temperature, the remaining unmelted block is removed.

In the second method (where the same temperatures as the previous method are the rule), a third portion of melted chocolate is heated to the proper temperature, poured over a marble surface and stirred constantly with a flexible spatula or scraper until it begins to harden (without forming lumps or curdling). The hardened chocolate is added to the melted chocolate and stirred until cooled to the

Slice the butter into small chunks and melt in a heavy-duty saucepan over low heat or in a bain-marie. Once the butter has melted, remove from heat and allow to set for a few minutes, in order for the solids to settle to the bottom of the pan. Skim the foam from the surface and pour the clarified butter into a clean jar, making sure the solids remain at the bottom of the pan. Clarified butter keeps indefinitely in the refrigerator in a sealed jar.

Coconut milk

1 cup

Ingredients
- 1 coconut

Special equipment
- electric juicer

Preparation
Although canned coconut milk can be used in these recipes, you get a better flavor with fresh coconut. Peel the coconut, remove the flesh, and process in a juicer until obtaining the milk. One coconut yields about one cup

Coffee tuiles

Yields 8 to 10 *tuiles*

Ingredients
- 1 oz butter
- 1/3 cup confectioners' sugar
- 1 tablespoon instant coffee
- 2 tablespoons corn syrup
- 1/3 cup sifted flour
- 1 tablespoon hot water

Special equipment
- kitchen scales
- measuring cup
- pastry bag fitted with a small tip
- *silpat* sheet

Preparation
Cream the butter, sugar, and the coffee together; beat until creamy. Add the corn syrup, flour, and hot water. Continue beating until batter is smooth. One cannot stress enough that the dough must be homogeneous.
Chill for one hour.
Preheat the oven to 300°F/150°C.
With a pastry bag fitted with a small tip, pipe out ten coils onto a *silpat* sheet and bake until golden. Remove from oven and, while the coils are hot, roll them freehand, holding them in your hands until cooled.

Keep in an airtight container until serving.

Coffee tuiles make a delicious accompaniment to ice creams, custards and *crème fraîche*.

Crème anglaise

Yields 1 liter

Ingredients
- 4 cups milk
- 5 egg yolks
- 1¼ cup sugar
- 1 teaspoon vanilla extract

Special equipment
- measuring cup

Preparation
Heat the milk until boiling; remove from heat. In a separate bowl, beat the egg yolks with the sugar and vanilla extract until pale and creamy. Slowly whisk the hot milk into the beaten egg yolks. Transfer to a heavy-duty saucepan and cook over low heat, stirring with a wooden spoon until the mixture coats the back of the spoon. Strain into a bowl set over an ice bath and cool.

Italian meringue

Yields 600g

Ingredients
- ½ cup water
- 1¾ cup sugar
- 1 oz corn syrup
- 6 egg whites

Special equipment
- kitchen scales
- measuring cup
- electric beater

Preparation
In a heavy-duty saucepan, mix the water, sugar, and corn syrup. Cook over high heat until the mixture reaches 250°F/121°C, or the hard ball stage.
Skim all the foam floating from the top, and with a wet pastry brush, clean the rim of the pan. With an electric mixer, beat the egg whites until foamy. Reduce the speed to low and pour the syrup in a thin trickle over the beaten egg whites. Once all the syrup has been blended in, increase the speed to high and continue beating until the mixture cools completely, about five minutes.

Kiwi parfait glacé

Yields 2 cups

Ingredients
- 2 leaves of gelatin
- 2 tablespoons water
- ½ cup sugar
- 1 teaspoon lemon juice
- 4 egg yolks
- 4 kiwis, peeled and sliced, core removed
- 1 and ¼ cup heavy cream, well chilled

Special equipment
- measuring cup

Preparation
Soak the gelatin in iced water until softened.
In a heavy-bottomed pan, heat the water, the sugar and the lemon juice until boiling. With a wet pastry brush, clean the rim of the pan to prevent the sugar from crystallizing. Cook until the syrup reaches 250°F/121°C or the hard ball stage.
Beat the egg yolks. Whisking constantly, add the syrup in a thin trickle. Beat until the mixture cools thoroughly.
Cut the kiwis in pieces, and purée in the blender. Drain the gelatin, heat gently in a saucepan until dissolved, and stir into the purée. Gently stir in the beaten egg yolks. With an electric mixer, whisk the

chilled cream until it forms soft peaks. Gently fold the whipped cream into the rest of the preparation. Cover with plastic wrap and store in the refrigerator.

Light syrup

Yields 2 cups

Ingredients
- 2 cups water
- 2 cups sugar

Special equipment
- measuring cup

Preparation
In a heavy-duty saucepan, heat the water with the sugar until completely dissolved. Remove from heat and cool.

Little lemon halves

Yields 40 pieces

Ingredients
- 20 lemons, rinsed well
- pinch baking soda
- 6 cups water
- 2 cups sugar

Special equipment
- measuring cup

Preparation
Cut the lemons in half and remove the pulp, taking care not to pierce the rinds. Put the rinds in a large, nonreactive pot, cover with water, and add the baking soda. Boil briefly and strain, discarding the water. In a large bowl, copper-lined, heat the water with the sugar. Add the lemon halves and cook over low heat for one hour. Remove from heat and cool. Preserve the lemon rinds in the syrup.

Mint cream filling

Yields 1 1/2 cups

Ingredients
- 1/2 leaf of gelatin
- 1/8 cup sugar
- 3 egg yolks
- 1 cup heavy cream
- 20 mint leaves
- 2 tablespoons *crème de menthe*

Special equipment
- measuring cup

Preparation
Soak the gelatin in iced water until softened.
In a heavy-duty saucepan, mix the sugar with the egg yolks, and put in a bain-marie. Do not let the water temperature exceed 120°F/50°C. Beat constantly with an electric or manual beater, until the mixture swells and doubles in volume.
The mixture must heat only slightly.
Remove from the heat. Heat the cream with the mint leaves, without letting boil. Remove from the heat and cool for ten to twelve minutes. Strain, discarding the mint leaves, and add the *crème de menthe*. Stir well. Drain the gelatin carefully and dissolve in three tablespoons of the hot cream.

Whisk this into the rest of the
warm cream. Slowly whisk
the cream into the beaten
egg yolks.
Chill until thoroughly chilled.

Puff pastry

Yields 3 lb of pastry dough

Ingredients
- 4 cups wheat flour
- 1 cup water
- 1 tablespoon salt
- 1/4 cup melted butter
- 14 oz chilled butter

Special equipment
- kitchen scales
- measuring cup

Preparation
Sift the flour into a deep bowl
or onto a working surface.
Add the water, salt and
melted butter, and knead
until dough is smooth. Shape
the dough into a ball and
slash a cross cut on top. Wrap
the dough in plastic wrap
and cool in the refrigerator
for at least one hour. Place
the chilled butter between
two sheets of waxed paper.
Beat then roll out with a
rolling pin until forming a
square 1cm thick. Return the
butter to the refrigerator to
chill. When the dough has
cooled, transfer to a work
surface lightly sprinkled with
flour. With a rolling pin, roll
out the four sides of the cross
until the dough is an even
thickness of 1.5cm. Place the
butter square in the center of
the cross and wrap in the
cross, taking care not to let
any butter show. Refrigerate
for 15 minutes. Return the
dough to the lightly floured
work surface. Roll the dough
out with a rolling pin, working
in the same direction, until
forming a rough 30x60cm
rectangle. Fold the dough in
three to form a smaller
rectangle. Repeat the rolling
and folding once more. Wrap
the dough in plastic wrap
and refrigerate for at least
one hour. Fold again twice, in
the same manner as before,
and chill for another hour.
Repeat the operation one last
time: the dough has now
been folded six times. The
puff pastry is now ready to
be used. It is advisable to
divide it into smaller portions
to make your job easier.
Spread the puff pastry to the
thickness indicated in the
recipe, and chill for a few
minutes before slicing. This
ensures a neater cutting and

Raspberry coulis

Yields 1/2 cup

Ingredients
- 3 1/2 oz raspberries
- 1 tablespoon sugar
- 1/2 lemon

Special equipment
- kitchen scales

Preparation
Purée the raspberries in the
blender with the sugar and
the lemon juice; strain. Cover
with plastic wrap and store
covered in the refrigerator.

Rose ice cream

Yields 1 liter

Ingredients
- 1 cup milk
- 1 cup rose water
- 1 cup heavy cream
- 5 egg yolks
- 3/4 cup sugar

Special equipment
- measuring cup
- ice cream machine

Preparation
In a saucepan, heat the milk with the rose water.
In a bowl, beat the egg yolks with the sugar until pale and creamy. Add half the heavy cream; mix well. Slowly whisk the hot milk into the beaten egg yolks and cream. Transfer to a heavy-duty saucepan and cook over low, moderate heat. Stir constantly, patiently with a wooden spoon, without letting boil, until the foam disappears completely from the surface and the mixture coats the back of the spoon. Remove from heat and strain into bowl set over an ice bath. Add the rest of the cream and mix well. Allow to cool for ten to twelve minutes, then chill thoroughly in the refrigerator. Pour into an ice cream machine and process according to the manufacturer's instructions. Store in the freezer until serving.

Strawberry mousse

Yields 4 cups

Ingredients
- 1/2 leaf of gelatin
- 2 cups strawberries, washed, stems removed
- 2 cups heavy cream
- 3 tablespoons sugar

Special equipment
- measuring cup

Preparation
Soak the gelatin in iced water until softened.
Halve the strawberries and purée in the blender. Measure out two cups. Drain the gelatin and heat gently until dissolved. Add the strawberry purée and whisk in thoroughly. In a deep bowl, beat the cream with the sugar until it forms soft peaks. Gently fold in the strawberry purée. Cover with plastic wrap, cool, and store in the refrigerator.

Vanilla crème anglaise

Yields 250g

Ingredients
- 1 whole vanilla bean
- 2 cups milk
- 5 egg yolks
- 3/4 cup sugar
- 1/8 cup sifted flour
- 1/8 cup corn starch
- 2/3 oz butter

Special equipment
- kitchen scales
- measuring cup

Preparation
With a paring knife, slice the vanilla bean lengthwise and scrape out the seeds with the back of the knife. Add the pod and seeds to the milk and heat until boiling. Remove from heat and discard the vainilla pod. In a bowl, beat the egg yolks with the sugar until pale and creamy. Whisk in the sifted flour and corn starch, beating constantly. Slowly whisk the hot milk into the mixture. Transfer to a heavy-duty saucepan and cook over low heat until thickened, whisking constantly. Remove from heat and stir in the butter, mixing thoroughly. Pour this cream into a bowl, cover with plastic wrap, cool, and store in the refrigerator.

Vanilla génoise

Yields one 30x40cm layer

Ingredients
- 5 eggs
- 5/8 cup sugar
- 1 teaspoon vanilla extract
- 1 cup sifted flour
- 1/8 cup melted butter, slightly cooled

Special equipment
- measuring cup
- 1 sheet pan 30x40cm
- *silpat* sheet, optional

Preparation
Preheat the oven to 350°F/ 175°C.

In a deep bowl, beat the eggs with the sugar and vanilla extract, until pale and creamy. Put in a bain-marie and beat constantly until the mixture doubles in volume. Do not let the water temperature exceed 120°F/ 50°C. Remove from bain-marie. Add the flour gradually to the beaten eggs, folding with a spatula. Mix the melted butter with a tablespoon of the batter and fold into the rest of the preparation. Take care not to beat excessively or the batter will deflate.

Pour over a greased and floured sheet pan or one that's lined with a *silpat* sheet, and spread the batter evenly with a metal spatula. Bake until lightly browned, about 10 minutes. Remove from oven and cool at room temperature.

Vanilla ice cream

Yields 1 liter

Ingredients
- 2 cups milk
- 2 vanilla beans
- 5 egg yolks
- 3/4 cup sugar
- 1 cup heavy cream

Special equipment
- measuring cup
- ice cream machine

Preparation
With a paring knife, slice the vanilla beans lengthwise. Scrape out the seeds with the back of the knife and add the pod, seeds, and milk in a saucepan. Heat until boiling and remove from heat, discarding the vanilla pod. In a bowl, beat the egg yolks with the sugar until pale and creamy. Add half the cream and mix well. Slowly whisk the hot milk into the beaten egg yolks and cream. Transfer to a heavy-duty saucepan and cook over low heat. Stir constantly with a wooden spoon, without letting boil, until the foam disappears from the surface and the mixture coats the back of the spoon. Remove from heat and strain into a bowl set over an ice bath. Add the rest of the cream and mix well. Cool, then chill thoroughly. Pour into an ice cream machine and proceed according to the manufacturer's directions. Store in the freezer until serving.

Walnut
ice cream

Yields 1 liter

Ingredients

- 2 cups milk
- 1 teaspooon walnut extract
- 5 egg yolks
- ³/₄ cup sugar
- 1 cup heavy cream
- ¹/₂ cup ground nuts

Special equipment

- measuring cup
- ice cream machine

Preparation

Heat the milk with the walnut extract.

Meanwhile, beat the egg yolks with the sugar until pale and creamy. Add half the cream and mix well. Gently stir the hot milk into the beaten egg yolks and cream. Transfer to a heavy-duty saucepan and cook over low heat. Stir constantly with a wooden spoon, without letting boil, until the foam disappears completely from the surface and the mixture coats the back of the spoon. Remove from heat and strain into a bowl set over an ice bath. Add the rest of the cream and mix well. Cool thoroughly in the refrigerator. Add the ground nuts. Pour into the ice cream machine and proceed accoding to the manufacturer's instructions. Store in the freezer until serving.

You can make interesting varieties by choosing different kinds of nuts, and using them alone or in creative, exotic blends.

Glossary

Agrás, *Vaccinium meridionale*

Also agraz. Small, dark purple berry, fruit of a wild vine species; native of bleak South American plateaus.

Al dente

Italian expression referring to an ideal cooking point for pasta and vegetables: still slightly firm or crunchy.

Amaretto

As *Amaretto di Saronno* is commonly known, an Italian liqueur made with almonds.

Angel hair

Caramelized sugar threads which are molded into various shapes.

Arequipe

Typical Colombian milk pudding.

Armagnac

Famous French dry brandy, distilled in the province of the same name.

Aspic

Firm-textured jelly, prepared from beef or fish stock, used to accompany or cover meats, seafood, eggs, pâtés, and other dishes.

Baba

Pastry of French origin with raisins; usually soaked in rum or brandy.

Bailey's Irish Cream

Brand name of a sweet Irish liqueur prepared with Irish whisky, heavy cream, and cocoa.

Bain-marie

A double set of pans and the form of cooking with them. The bigger pan, which contains water, is placed over heat. The smaller pan within contains the food or preparation to be cooked in "bain-marie". The smaller pan, which never is in direct contact with heat, receives constant gentle heat.

Bavarois

Popular French preparation, made with eggs, sugar, heavy cream and gelatin.

Blini

Small pancakes of Russian origin, usually accompanied by caviar and sour cream.

Brioche

Sweet, yeast-raised bread, enriched with butter and eggs.

Cassava

Tuber from the lower American tropics, staple food of many populations.

Cassis

Extract of a dark-purple berry of French origin, which is used in several preparations. One of the better-known is the sweet liqueur called *crème de cassis.*

Cellophane noodles

Noodles made from a type of bean, a common ingredient in soups, salads, and other preparations in south-east Asia. The Japanese name is *harusame.*

Cocada

A kind of soft nougat, prepared with sugar or *panela* (see below) and grated coconut. Extremely common on the Caribbean, Atlantic, and Pacific coasts of South America, wherever coconut grows.

Cognac

Dry brandy distilled and bottled in the French town and province of the same name.

Crème de menthe

A sweet mint-flavored liqueur, usually colored bright green.

Curry

Aromatic and pungent mixture of various spices, including cumin, coriander, pepper, and turmeric. Widely-used in Indian, Thai, and Indonesian cuisine.

Curuba, *Pasiflora mollisima*

Fruit of the *curubo,* a tropical climbing plant found only in Andean zones of Colombia and Bolivia. It is elliptic, of a color ranging from green to yellow and pale orange, and grows at between 6000 to 10 000 feet above sea level. Curuba blends especially well with milk, making delicious shakes. Rich in vitamin C and A, and phosphorus, it only has a sugar content of 6%.

Dubonnet

Brand name of a sweet, aromatized red or white wine, served traditionally as an *apéritif.*

Earl Grey

Type of tea spiced with extract of bergamot, a citrus common in the Mediterranean.

Feijoa, *Feijoa sellowiana*

Fruit of a small perennial namesake shrub, native to southern Brazil and Uruguay, widely used in juices, desserts, sponge cakes, and ice creams. It owes its name to Don José de Silva Feijo, botanist and curator of the Madrid's Museo de Historia Natural during the colonial period, and to Friedrich Sellow, German botanist who explored Brazil in the 19th century.

Ganache

French name for a mixture of chocolate and heavy cream; used for filling various types of chocolates and chocolate pastries.

Génoise

French term for a smooth and delicate cake, prepared with flour, eggs, sugar and butter. Génoise can be used as a base for desserts.

Granadilla, *Passiflora legularis*

Round ochre-yellow fruit with a hard, brittle skin, an opalescent, thick, slippery, fragrant pulp, and many small, edible, black seeds. It grows between 4000 and 8000 feet above sea level. It is the Colombian fruit *par excellence.*

Grand Marnier

Brand name of a well-known French liqueur prepared with orange extract and brandy.

Gratin

A preparation in sauce, covered with melted butter and breadcrumbs, that has been browned under the heat of the broiler.

Jasmine

Flower of the namesake shrub, native to Persia, widely used in perfumery.

Julienne

A preparation made by cutting fruit or vegetables into fine strips.

Kahlua

Brand name of a coffee liqueur often used in confectionery for making sweet fillings.

Kir royal

French cocktail prepared with champagne and *crème de cassis.*

Macadamia, *Macadamia ternifolia*

Native to Australia, this is a nut of very pleasant taste and similar size to the hazelnut.

Macaroon

Name of Italian origin, for a small and popular crisp cookie, made with almond paste or ground almonds, sugar and egg whites.

Mamoncillo, *Melicocca bijuga*

Small fruit of the namesake tree. The creamy, delicate pulp, is bright orange in color and has a juicy, velvety texture, and envelops a seed almost as large as the entire fruit.

Mascarpone

Thick, creamy cheese, native to the province of Lombardy, now produced throughout Italy.

Oblea

Paper-thin biscuit made with wheat flour and water, usually in hot presses. Perhaps its best-known form is the host, or consecrated wafer, for the Catholic sacrament of communion.

Panela

Colombian name for sugarloaf or solidified cane molasses, found in square or round blocks; highly popular ingredient of various drinks and preparations.

Papayuela, *Carica gouditiana*

Also known as wild papaya, the fruit has a yellow skin and fleshy pulp. Inedible raw, it is used for sweets and preserves.

Parfait

French name for a preparation made of heavy cream, gelatin, egg yolks, and sugar.

Pastis

Anissed liquor, highly popular in Provence and especially the region around Marseille.

Pâte sucrée

French name for a classic dough preparation, frequently used for *tartelette* crust.

Petit-beurre

Sweet cookie made with wheat flour and butter.

Petits pots de crème

French term for a kind of small flan made with heavy cream, made in several flavors.

Phyllo

Pastry prepared in extremely thin sheets; widely used in Greek and Middle-Eastern *pâtisserie.* Phyllo pastry can be rolled paper-thin and shaped into a wide variety of shapes and textures.

Pitahaya, *Hylocereus triangularis*

Tropical fruit of the cactus family, with a yellow, scaly peel, a delicate, translucent, white pulp, and crunchy black seeds. Rich in phosphorus, calcium and ascorbic acid, it grows best above 800m above sea level. There are approximately 18 varieties, from ochre to bright, dark red. The red pitahaya has less flavor.

Quenelle

French word of German etymology, *Knödel,* meaning boiled doughball. Sphere or cylinder-shaped. The English equivalent is dumpling. *Quenelles* are made most commonly made with fish, veal, chicken, and fowl livers.

Rodoid **plastic strips**

Disposable plastic sheets, used to prepare several varieties of chocolate, including tablets.

Roquefort

French cheese shot through with a bluish-green mold. Made of whole sheep's milk, native to Roquefort-sur-Soulzon, a small village in the south of France.

Sapodilla, *Matisia cordata*

Fruit native to the Colombian Andes. Sapodilla has a thick, dark grey skin, large seeds and fibrous, orange pulp. It only grows up to 5000 feet above sea level. Oil from the seeds was used by Mexican Indians to add flavor to chocolate.

Savarin

Mold for a sweet cake similar to a baba.

Soufflé

Classic French cuisine preparation, sweet or savory, made with egg whites and thickened with egg yolks.

Star anise

Spice native to China and south-east Asia, shaped like an eight-pointed star, with an unmistakable sweet licorice flavor.

Starfruit

Bright yellow, oblong South American fruit, star-shaped in diameter.

Strudel

Austrian dessert made of thin sheets of dough filled with fruit, or cheese and raisins.

Sushi

Of Japanese origin, these little rolls of vinegared rice are squeezed together by hand, topped by a slice of raw fish or seafood, and wrapped in seaweed.

Tamale

Widespread Latin American dish made with corn or rice filling, and stuffed with various spicy flavorings, wrapped in leaves from different trees (depending on the country); tamales are steamed or baked.

Tapioca

White, granular starch extracted from the cassava root.

Terrine

French name for the dish as well as the mold in which pâté or other mixtures of meat or vegetables are prepared.

Tree tomato, *Cyphomandra betacea*

Fruit of a shrub native to the high Andes in Colombia, Peru, Ecuador, Bolivia and Chile. It has a smooth skin of a color ranging from orange to deep red, and a striking ellipsoid shape. Seeds resemble those of the common tomato. Rarely eaten raw, it is mostly used in the preparation of juices, sweets, and preserves. In Colombia it grows between 1,000 and 3,000m above sea level. Extremely rich in vitamin A.

Tuile

French term for a variety of thin cookies used for constructing pastries, desserts, and savory dishes of all sorts.

Uchuva, *Physalis peruviana*

Yellow, round fruit of the *uchuvo,* a wild tropical shrub found in certain parts of Latin America. A remarkable characteristic of the *uchuva* is that it is wrapped in a leafy envelope which protects it from blights and insects. Used in juices, ice creams, preserves and salads. Extremely rich in vitamin A.

Wasabi

Hot, green, Japanese horseradish which sometimes comes in powder form.

Zabaglione

Italian custard mixture of eggs and sugar used to soak certain preparations and which can be flavored with liqueurs. In French known as *sabayon.*

pecial equipment

Special utensils frequently used in the preparation of the desserts in this book.

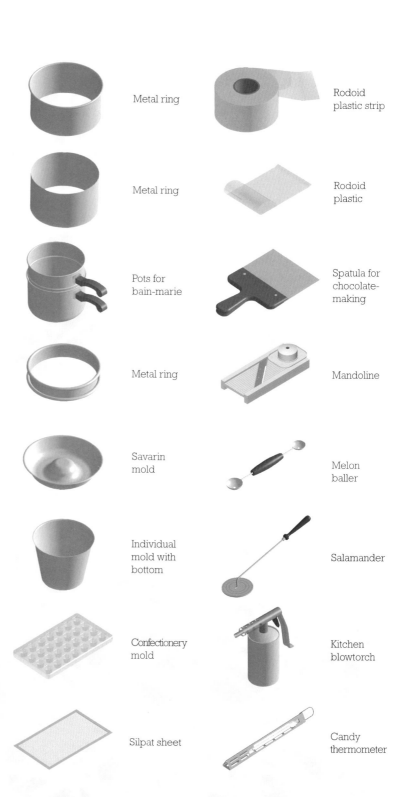

Metal ring

Metal ring

Pots for bain-marie

Metal ring

Savarin mold

Individual mold with bottom

Confectionery mold

Silpat sheet

Wire cake rack

Rodoid plastic strip

Rodoid plastic

Spatula for chocolate-making

Mandoline

Melon baller

Salamander

Kitchen blowtorch

Candy thermometer

Hook for electric beater

Indexes

Index of
desserts by
names

Index by names of recipes